STARTING RUMORS
America's Next Generation of Writers

STARTING RUMORS
America's Next Generation of Writers

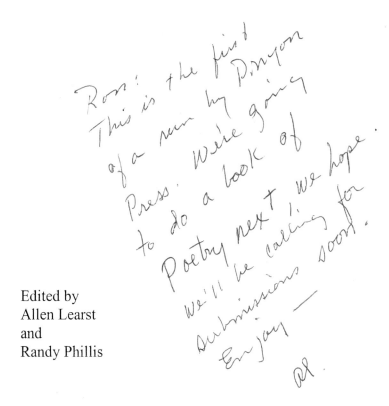

Ron: This is the first of a new by Pinyon Press. We're going to do a book of Poetry next! We hope We'll be calling for submissions soon. Enjoy —

Al.

Edited by
Allen Learst
and
Randy Phillis

PINYON PRESS   GRAND JUNCTION

First Published in 1999 by
Pinyon Press
Languages, Literature and Communications
Mesa State College
Grand Junction CO 81502

ISBN 09671216-0-4

PRINTED IN THE UNITED STATES OF AMERICA

CONTENTS

STARTING RUMORS
America's Next Generation of Writers

FOREWORD

Even in the most contemporary of anthologies it seems we've begun to see the same names over and over. This is only natural, as the baby-boom generation matures and their writings are at the fore-front of the literary scene. There is, however, a new generation of writers emerging, the so-called Generation-X, born between the years 1965 and 1976. These writers are also publishing books and appearing in anthologies. What perhaps separates this group is their concerns and views of the world.

Our goal in this collection is to give this group a voice that can be accessed in a single volume. Formally, their work holds affinity with that of their slightly older peers, sometimes traditional, sometimes innovative; their perspectives are equally authentic. Beyond that, we leave it to the readers to reach their own conclusions.

We are privileged to present this fine writing to you, and hope you find it a pleasurable and enlightening reading experience.

The Man Who Wouldn't Plant Willow Trees

A.E. STALLINGS

Willows are messy trees. Hair in their eyes,
They weep like women after too much wine
And not enough love. They litter a lawn with leaves
Like the butts of regrets smoked down to the filter.

They are always out of kilter. Thirsty as drunks,
They'll sink into a sewer with their roots.
They have no pride. There's never enough sorrow.
A breeze threatens and they shake with sobs.

Willows are slobs, and must be cleaned up after.
They'll bust up pipes just looking for a drink.
Their fingers tremble, but make wicked switches.
They claim they are sorry, but they whisper it.

A Lament for the Dead Pets of our Childhood

A.E. STALLINGS

Even now I dream of rabbits murdered
By loose dogs in the dark, the saved-up voice
Spilt on that last terror, or the springtime
Of lost baby rabbits, grey and blind
As moles, that slipped from birth and from the nest
Into a grey, blind rain, became the mud.
And still I gather up their shapes in dreams,
Those poor, leftover Easter eggs, all grey.

That's how we found out death: the strangled bird
Undone by a toy hung in his cage,
The foundlings that would never last the night
Be it pigeon, crippled snake, the kitten
Whose very fleas forsook it in the morning
While we nursed a hangover of hope.

After the death of pets, dolls lay too still
And wooden in the cradle, sister, after
We learned death: not hell, no ghosts or angels,
But a cold thing in the image of a warm thing,
Limp as sleep without the twitch of dreams.

Insomnia

–and some say it's like the calm after the storm.
Whereas others insist on the morality of the thing.
There are those who will tell you it's the cat's fault, or the fire
                                                           station's.
And those who believe it's a motor inn on wheels that travels
faster than the
        speed of light.
A famous mathematician wants to solve its matrix, must
approximate due to the
        lack of concrete boundaries.
Nine people are writing the definitive book on it.
Some college student, thinking it a highball, orders a shot of
it.
Fortune tellers everywhere rely on it for advice.
Three dogs–all Doberman Pincers–share its name, as does
                            one young girl, from
    Omaha.
A kid forgot what it was until it came to him bared and
gleaming. He remembered it then–he hasn't known anything
                            else since–

The Man in Uniform, or: Why Women Should Drink Milk

JILL CRAMMOND

How we wish we'd had a milkman,
sigh the women of today. A smiling
all-American man, working his way

through our neighborhood in trim-
lined trousers and a smart sailor cap.
Winding through alleys, over hedges,

around gates, crisp and quick in his chalk-
white uniform, he would swiftly deliver
us his shining glass prize–rigidly

upright, cream foaming in frozen bursts
on the ridged lips of each red stamped
bottle. And when our milk was gone, our

carafes cleansed and empty, the milkman would
appear, laden on our shaded porches, with
wire baskets full of his magic liquid.

Little Boy Lost, 1970

JOE CLARK

A boy through snow
to home from kindergarten
loses his paper silhouette
to winter breeze.
He chases clumsy in heavy gear
until his leg falls through ice.
He runs home with stiff shin,
enters screaming,
"Mommy, I lost *me*, Mommy.
I lost me."
He leads her by the hand
to the shore where the wind
picked up, where he held
the thick paper toward sky
and the air tore it from his hand,
sent it onto barely frozen lake.
One mitten grips
his mother's fingers,
the other points
to a field
where legs fall vulnerable.
Somewhere torn,
black construction paper
in the shape of this boy
with a barely upturned nose
and tiny cowlick
clings to the slow freeze of slush
under the weight of falling snow.

You Sat with Kittens
for Linda, my stepmother

JOE CLARK

You sat with kittens
curled and shivering at your feet,
and you fed the dying
from a doll's bottle
until his wiry hair
and spider body
grew full and fat.
You made the cold go away,
made the damp,
plastic interior
of January crashed
and abandoned Chevrolet,
kittens climbing frozen kittens
to rub swollen paws
against shattered glass,
a thing of kitty history.
And today they walk
like I do– head high,
in and out,
noses pressed against
the refrigerator.
But unlike the kittens,
you can be sure that I remember
when the wind blew cold,
how my ear froze stiff as ice
And I know how warm
the oil in the spoon was
when you touched the cotton
to it, and I hear as I did then

when you tipped my head
to put the soft fluid in,
the frozen river
begin to flow again.

Candy

JOE CLARK

Jerry always tried to ditch me,
tried to go to the Deli
without me, said to the new kid on the block
"Do you want to go to the D-E-L-I,"
but I wouldn't put up with it;
I couldn't spell, but the Deli
was the only place we went,
the only place to go
and I told him that Mom said he couldn't
go without out me,
so I had to walk fast and tired
behind him while he ran, skipped,
and played games with the new kid.

To Koetz's Deli was seven blocks,
on the corner of Genoa Ave, the only
two lane road in the village,
and Capillo, the road that led
to Johnson's Tavern on the beach
and the Fourth Lake Resort
where the Pollocks spent their weekends
away from Chicago.
And I didn't mind lagging behind
because I didn't like the new kid
because the day before he pushed
my face into ground and asked me if I liked
how the grass tasted.
And I didn't mind when my brother and him turned
around and stomped toward me,
with their arms and legs frantic
until they pointed to the ground in back of my shoes
and yelled, "LOOK OUT.
THE MOLECULES ARE BEHIND YOU,"
though I got red and jumped toward them looking for a hug.

22

I didn't mind because I was looking forward to candy,
and nothing they could do would stop
me from getting a whole bunch of it.
At the Deli there were boxes full
of giant candy bars: Butterfingers,
Kit Kats, Heath, Skor, the crunchy cookie kind;
and Pay Day, Snickers, Oh' Henry, the nutty kind I liked.
The Deli had jars of suckers:
Blow Pops, Tootsie Pops, Ring Pops, Dumb Dumbs.
And the hard to chew stuff like Bit-O-Honeys, Laffey
Taffey, Now & Laters, Tootsie Rolls, Rollos. Mini hard
                                                    candies
I'd pour in my hand like cereal: Nerds, Zots, Dweebs, Power
Pebbles. Gummie stuff like Dots, Cinnamon Bears, Worms,
                                                    little
gummie Riffle Rangers and Giant Red Rats.
And they had yard-long straws filled with Rainbow sugar
that made my mouth sweat, tangy, and dry.
They had licorice like fishing wire,
wire I could tie the plastic pig
my brother gave me
to the Hickory in my yard
and throw lit fire crackers at it.

And when we came out of the Deli
we'd swap gum–a Hubba Bubba
for a Tidal Wave, Lemon Bubblicious
for Cherry, the best for blowing bubbles.
On the way home I'd suck and slurp, and stuff
my pockets with wrappers.
Hard candy was my favorite,
and I always saved the butterscotch coin for tomorrow
when there'd be nothing else left.
I'd put a grape globe into my mouth,
press it against the roof with my tongue,
roll it around and slurp
until it was small enough to bite
or until it grew a sharp hole

that began to tear into my tongue
and my lips and I'd have to do away with it:
crush it in one hard bite,
a crackle storm under the weight
of my teeth. Sugar inside a cage
of wet flesh. It flavored my sputum
and made sweet the swallows.

II

Today the Deli's gone. Gone out of business.
And our families only have stories
about what a great lady Mrs. Koetz was,
her husband in a wheelchair.
One day Dad went in with $.72 to buy a few slices
of boiled ham, and Mrs. Koetz kept slicing
after Dad said, "that's enough...that's enough.
Mrs. Koetz that's enough, I've only got $.72,"
but she said, "It's O.K....you've got babies
to feed. Have some of my bread, too."

And then there's Marvin.
The youngest of the Longtons family
whose last name was Knuth.
Mrs. Koetz loved him, but he broke her heart.
When he was six, he stole a stack
of *Penthouses*, *Hustlers*, and *Swanks* from his old man,
and he set them in a rusty radio flyer
under the weight of a cinder block
that held a sign, "$.25." He went around the neighborhood
with a smile and an empty coffee can
until Mrs. Williams brought him home
to where his mother was sleeping.
Then Marvin got on the next door neighbor's bicycle
and he went to the Deli,
parked the bike in the back
and grabbed a case of empty 16oz. Pepsi
bottles from a giant stack that was ready for pick up.

24

Then he brought them in the front door
and said, "Mrs. Koetz, these are returns,"
and she gave him money to buy candy with,
and he did that twice a week
never knowing Mrs. Koetz knew all along
that she was giving it away. But he went too far.
The day Marvin
came in wearing a blue Spider Man ski mask,
waving a pellet gun up at her face,
after he shot a giant jar of dill pickles,
shot it again, shattered it to pieces,
and pickles fell to the counter then slid to the floor,
Mrs. Koetz took her husband to Florida.

I saw Marvin that evening,
and never asked
where he got all of that candy.
We hooked up with Michael Hoover,
a southern red-headed kid who usually wanted to kick my ass
but this day he stole some pot from his parents
and we went to the duck farm to smoke it.
I was seven, and Marvin told me not to tell my brothers
because they would beat him up.
We sat on a slope next to the woods,
a slope like the ones we climbed and played war on,
slopes of duck shit stirred in with woodchips.
We passed a joint between us
and tossed M & Ms into the air.

III

Marvin slit his wrists six years later,
two days after his brother, John,
got killed by a snow-plow
seconds after he dumped his motorcycle on an ice patch

25

in the middle of Genoa Ave.
But Marvin lived and today he's doing alright,
drives a custom '78 Trans Am
and sells cocaine.

But I won't touch the stuff.
My teeth grind as it is.
I work days at the junior high,
Lake Villa Intermediate,
and when I sleep at night I don't sleep,
and my wife, Karen, is concerned.
My bed is awkward. We make love
and then I lie on top of the blankets, wonder,
try to wonder about nothing after I've wondered for long
                                                                        enough
about the ocean, dusty hallways, carpets I've cleaned,
what on earth everybody I know is doing.
All night I press my jaw, continual,
not to chew and swallow her flavor
but to grind away the peaks of molars,
to make it easier to prod with swollen tongue
the valleys of nervous bone,
to prod and dig with the point
and rake with the edge of my tongue
to surface some lost sweet bit
ot broken Hollywood glass, some sweet bit of globe
sunk and lost deep in my teeth.

The years and years of this will flatten my molars.
But my brothers tell me nothing changes,
that we're still the same punks we were fifteen years ago,
only we're not young punks, we're old punks,
which means we have jobs.
I push a broom and empty trash all day.
I take dust out from under lockers, and occasionally
I get up to the roof and fetch lost balls
for the kids who've handed me a list.
But Allen says it doesn't mean jobs;

26

he says being an old punk
means having the experience
that young punks don't.
Like how he can roll a joint tighter,
like how he can roll it without taking his eyes
from a re-run of Home Improvement
while his daughters stay in their room
wearing stained Easter dresses in June
and smush crayons one by one into the door lock.
And for Nick it means having a lifetime supply of Rolaids
to go with his lifetime supply of Subway coupons.
Which means he knows how to live week to week
without putting more than five bucks in a gas tank
or a quarter in a pool table.
My other brother, Jerry, spends weekends
downtown away from his wife,
company business in the C-I-T-Y.
For all of us it means a golf cart
full of Old Style, a pack of smokes with at least two joints,
Cherry Coke, Captain Morgan's,
and plenty of balls so we don't have to look
for any in the trees or the corn fields
at the cheap-ass, nine-hole, dirt course
off of Hainseville Road.

For me it means a quick nap in the supply room
next to the gymnasium every day at lunch
when the faculty and students are on the other side
of the school. And sometimes I open the vending machine,
get myself some Recees to go with my coffee
when I wake up. Sometimes I go to the storage room
above the east annex, filter through year books
from when I was a student. I look at the tropheys
that don't belong to me, the ones thrown in boxes because
there's no room for display.
I sink my fingers deep in dust,
count the years on the plaques, the photographs
of old principals, teachers, coaches, teams.

It's 1997 and it seems
I've been staying after school
everyday since I was eight
to erase and clean the blackboards.

IV

The years of this flattens my teeth,
and when I look into my wife's eyes
I know that while we grow old together
the flavor of her falls each morning
when I spit out my taste buds
scraped knife clean by the prodding, scraping,
rolling, scraping, and grinding from the night before.

When I'm not sleeping
and my teeth are chewing themselves away,
I sometimes walk the hallways and try to think of nothing.
I move slowly with a soft broom in front of me
until there's a huge pile of pink dust.
At times I've seen myself waist high in the dust,
and I've been trampled by kids on their way to home-room.
I think of where it began, things my mother
told me never to eat before I go to bed.
I think of the wrappers left on the tables
in the commons. The boxes of candy
that go into the machines, how much dust cardboard produces.
And I imagine a giant brick,
a baseball bat, a snow-plow's blade hovering
inches above my face. Waiting to show me
how to think of nothing.

I only learn by walking the hallways.
That's what I tell myself each day,
each day while I wipe everything clean.
I go through these phrases in my head,
and I've learned to at least keep my shoulders relaxed
while I move through the school.

I go through these phrases, and I know
I have a few decades
before my tongue falls
completely dumb, before I understand
the Pollocks screaming at their children in underwear,
running ankle high in the water
chasing minnows, or before I understand why the biology
teacher in the North hallway smiles at me each morning
and ignores me when I tilt my hat in the afternoon.
But I know that when I understand this,
when it finally happens
I'll be sitting across from my grandfather,
the clock he gave me,
and my eyes will be giant and stiff–
solid red like Gob Stoppers
and wide for visitors to see as my head
tilts to the sway of the butterscotch pendulum,
and they will listen to the sound
I try to hear every night,
the sound my head will make after Karen
pushes a vitamin past
my parted lips where it will drop and roll
from wall of broken teeth
to wall of broken teeth.
The sound of the years before gravity pulls it to a dissolve,
the slide and click of a coin back and forth
inside a shoebox.

August Snowstorm
Kansas, 1874

JAMIE SIMPSON

The fields developed into acres of golden loneliness,
Not a weed to be seen in all the tassel, perfect.
To us it looked like payment for all the years
We scrabbled in the hard dirt, praying
Each time we sowed a seed for it to grow.
The neighbors rode to our sod home
And we all ate boiled buffalo and apple sass.
They told tales of the next town where trains
Could not start or stop because the tracks
Were slick with mangled grasshoppers.

That afternoon, in a haze of white vapor,
Millions of mirrored wings caught sunbeams.
They began dropping near twilight,
Three or four inches deep, snapping tree limbs
Under their weight, striking the ground with a sound
Like hail. They ate every green thing, and more.
You could feel your clothes unraveling as they pulled
The green threads out of the weave, out of your life.

Spectators

JAMIE SIMPSON

We raised our hands to shield
Our eyes when she jumped.
Always the girl quick to kiss,
She knew a single red ribbon
Could make you beautiful.
But she got silent and hungry
Like the middle of the night.
We only heard the razor,
Saw dark hair slide in sheets
To the floor like the loosened robe
Of a lover coming to bed.
We thought to reach out
And feel her forehead for fever,
But only made the sign of the cross.
She threw her hair out the window,
Watched it sail, sink down.
She sat in the windowsill
Cooing, scanning the horizon.
Thinking thoughts
Too thin to understand.
We stared at her out on the railing
And thought that she might
Blow us a kiss, wave.

On Viewing Police Photographs of New York's 1915 Homicides

Stasis
the bodies

Time passing casts off particles of itself:
images, documents, relics, junk.
Among these are dissertations never read,
codes undeciphered, objects of particular import
never understood, and traces of beings lost
to history without monument or memory,

just a name somewhere in an official record.
Each day a scattering of researchers
investigate faint footprints in microfilm.
A montage of murder multiplies,
pinned specimens of an extinguished race.
Endless negative copies of precinct blotters

in spidery copperplate script eternally record
drunk-and-disorderly charges against
forgotten persons on forgotten nights.
Mass temporarily situated represents the void,
raising knots anew for evidence
of the permanence of print, tag or optic lens.

Flux
The lives

Often, their tiny rooms fully dressed
with complex figured wallpaper,
threadbare but ornate carpets
laid over equally complex linoleum,
and curtains, flounces, doilies, runners.
What had they done the day before?

In life, they would have all worn hats.
These hats came off when they were shot
at card games, at dances, after being thrown out
of dances, tossed from taxicabs, beaten to death
on Wall Street. Disputes closed in blood;
Supine figures mark a greater care.

Every bit of space bears an image.
What leads us all to the mean bedrooms
and vacant lots and barroom floors
where we finish? Many love obliterated.
Entranced by lives we stumbled into,
we corner the landlady for unbloodied bedding.

Guest Stars

Sweeping the scope across the sky,
I try to find supernova remnants:
The Veil Nebula in Cygnus,
The Rig in Lyra, or the Eskimo.
I crave this delicate networking
That looks so much like spider's lace.

I imagine you dream of these explosions,
More luminous than our sun,
Creating shock waves in space.
Blood pounding, you create them in me,
Heavy and regular as a pulsar.

We owe our existence to large masses
Blowing themselves apart;
Their energy creating all the elements,
Flowing through space to collect here.

Everything hinges on the nucleus of a star
Falling to the center as its core collapses.
But this is not predictable; we must wait.

You shift everything into focus,
Show me the dimensions.
Inside the lens there is glowing
The same pale green as your eyes,
A double star formation, a nice find.

34

Gratitude

SEAN THOMAS DOUGHERTY

A morning without work is a morning to breathe, to watch the
rain clear and walk inside the passing voices of strangers, a
dog's barking, students with their bouncing knapsacks of
books, baseball hats worn backwards, as I walk headed toward
nowhere important, which is, of course, the most important
place of all–the trees dazzling with light, the dog laps a puddle
reflecting the sky, drinking the shimmer, his belly a puddle of
sky, and my feet beginning to glide down the block, children
skipping rope on the sidewalk, hip hopping to hop scotch calls
and Double Dutch dance steps, scrawling their names in wet
chalk running colors like a clown's extravagant tears–the
minor miracle of my job, this gathering and giving of details:
A woman's perfume, lilacs and lemons, the breath of a baby's
hair.

On The South Side

SEAN THOMAS DOUGHERTY

Someone fires a gun
after dark
beneath a streetlight
it a spark of flame
that echoes sirens
in the park

where boys play ball,
the park where every hoop's a streetlight's
bulb, as cops with hands on guns
hassle winos, light the dark
with flashlight flames,
the sirens

sing, the sirens
spin their threads, wake the dead, *gun*
every mother thinks, the dark
sounds with switches flicked, the streetlights
shudder, the park
fills with detectives, flames

from sirens, flames
that blaze the trees, the park
a circle of sirens,
cops search for the gun
that broke the streetlight's
silence, the dark

that speaks, the dark
that breathes the flames
of arson fires, the park
at night where sirens shriek,
where guns
are drawn beneath a streetlight's

sorrow, a streetlight's net of light, sirens
raining flames
that burn the parks
on summer nights, the dark
that signals curfew, a gun

in the park, before the sirens
flame the dark, the streetlights
flicker on, someone draws his gun.

A Fair Share of Morning

JACK B. BEDELL

Through the shadow of his face on the glass
he watches two deer rub necks
in the herb garden out back.
They bump against each other gently and graze
through the rows of thyme and basil.
His own breakfast pops in the skillet
behind him; the afternoon's turkey
sweats in the oven stirring the cat
towards the door. He has beaten the sun
to all this again so waits
for its light to crawl over his hill.
He knows he will have to wake the woman
soon, but lets her sleep for now
while she grows by the minute
into something that breathes for them both.
For this, he wonders if his fair share
is to wake early and slide food
onto warmed plates, to straighten
things and speak softly around her.
The creaks of their mattress answer him.
As he sets the meal beside the bed
she rolls toward him with a yawn
and pulls back the covers to show
how her stomach grows in the fresh sun,
reflects his grin like the back of a spoon
stretching him over itself.
He strums her shoulder and opens his mouth
to begin a promise that's going to take
a lifetime to finish out.

To See You as You Are, I

CHRISTINE L. MONAHAN

would have to spelunk into that cave, your throat,
walk backwards down its rock wall, say
Ah, stalactites,
and become distracted from my fear of the dark.

Or, I could peer into your ear,
letting the ear-cup suck over one eye-socket,
sealing out intrusive light.
Purple crystal would appear to me then,
I'd whisper, *Amethyst!,*
pleased to find a city of gems, undisclosed by the exterior of
your bowed head,
ordinary
as biscuit-brown quartz.

Yet, a kaleidoscope might turn within you,
and I would shut my free eye,
hard,
so that the Sun could shuffle your colors, while I'd wait
to be dealt a full hand
of tropical plumage
in the casino of light.

In fact, if I looked long enough I'm sure I would see that
stained-glass spins inside you:
Mourning Mother Mary falls forward,
baby-blue veil drops
onto the fleecy back of the gold-crowned Lamb of God,
rolling head-first toward the
Stations of the Cross
in reverse,
Saint Sebastian's bare body bends
blooming arrow-points,

then it somersaults,
and handsprings
steadily
into my iris.

Beard Lady's Circus

LAURA LEE WASHBURN

In this show we have a white barn duck.
The duck is quiet. He sits on straw.
I bought him for a good price
all right. Figured if he didn't work out,
one night we'd have duck for dinner.
The smallest small person clown can cook.
He's one hell of a cook, does a lot with game.

But I like this duck. I've made him,
given him his own legend.
He's The White Duck from Indiana,
the one who fucked a widow
right there at the edge of her own
backyard. In Indiana, that story don't wash. I tell you
that duck'll leave beak marks,
peanut bruises on your neck.

I'd like to get together with that duck
sometime for the show. We'd be good again.
That Indiana woman was too ordinary,
like someone's Aunt Rose. She belonged
in that Indiana town, not on the road
with my duck. Otherwise, you know,
the duck would've stuck with her.
A silver leash around his neck, that duck
struts. Two strong men pretend
to hold him back. That duck don't fool me.

We have him trained–one time
I wore metal over my tits
and walked out in front of him.
The duck went crazy. He lifted his wings,

41

let them spread out into their full wingspan,
two long white shafts of flight, lifting.
He made duck noises, and then, Mercy,
the dick came out. It was real.

Now we let him fake it with a woman.
Someone rushes with a cape to cover her.

We leave one metal tip showing.
I bill the show, "For Married Men Only,"
and a disclaimer in red paint says,
"Some sensibilities may be offended."
This really pulls the suckers in.
I have the barker call out,
"Women Beware." He tells them
to stay far from this tent
of the wild and mighty Indiana duck
that has built up a taste for women partners.
I myself have started a rumor
that the duck sleeps each night
in my trailer loose. I keep him here
with me on purpose. This duck's valuable.
Let people think what they will.

Dying

LAURA LEE WASHBURN

The boy holds a dead brown moth
in his dirty fist.
He has dirt on him
as only children can.

All together
in one corner of the cold stairwell
are the bodies of twenty
or so brown dead moths.

Only the boy thinks to lift them up
and send them flying
between his thumb and finger.
He knows there might be something sad,
but he isn't sure what.

A woman told him
that moths fly into fire,
but he can't imagine it
and doesn't believe her.
He says, No, they just go close
and come back out.

He is only four,
but his mother always remembers
he will die. She asks him
who he wants to live with
when Mommy and Daddy die.
She asks him what will happen
when he dies.

Sometimes she lets her company
in on his answers. *Tell everyone
you said you want the birds
to eat your body when you die.*
He reminds her he doesn't want to die.
If Mommy and Daddy die,
he will live with them,
he will save them,
they will not die.

In the corner of the cold stairwell
are the bodies of twenty or so
dead brown moths,
and some of them are small
like children. At home this boy
keeps a collection of rocks
on the window. One of them
has the shape of fish bones in it.

Lady bugs are outside
and also bugs that sting,
bugs he does not like,
and all around the driveway light,
the moths are circling up.
their cold wings lifting into light.

Fifteen Reasons We Can't Have an Intelligent Discussion About Gilligan's Island
for Bruce Taylor

PATTI SEE

You don't understand why any man wouldn't want to be king.
You think Hamlet shouldn't be a musical.
You never wanted to be Ginger but ended up the Professor.
You don't believe the cast is based on the seven deadly sins.

You don't know the Professor's name.
You've never contemplated why the Howells
took so much cash for a three hour trip.
You don't know where Mary Ann's from.

You're too contemporary to watch sitcoms that exploit
head hunters, near-sighted Japanese soldiers, and dyslexic
pilots.
You're too passive aggressive to watch a grown man
strike another with his captain's hat.

You wonder if Gilligan ever left his hammock
or why the Professor roomed alone.
You ponder what Skipper meant by Little Buddy.
You still haven't gotten over Maynard G. Krebbs'
cancellation.

You spent the seventies married
tying flies in your basement over a warm can of Schlitz.
I learned long division in front of the TV
humming *You're sure to get a smile*.

45

You spent the eighties at double bubble
rediscovering how to dance with a stranger.
I endured junior high's ugly years
with a predictable tune that soothed me through

dazed and clueless whistling each afternoon
This is a tale of our castaways.

When the Search Committee Asks Me To Tell a Little About Myself

PATTI SEE

I do not say
I like cottage cheese with pretzel rods
or pastrami on Wonder bread hold the mayo
like reading out loud to myself
and red grapes that squirt
don't say I inhaled, a lot.

Don't say how one March afternoon
a Sunday driving stoned with my best friend
in my father's yellow Delta '88 with the brown top
what she called my daisy mobile
I pierced an ear thick in cartilage
to chase away the munchies,

or say I feel bare
wearing my mother's pearl earrings
my own dotted studs and delicate hoops
worked out of cartilage
for the first time in ten years
left behind in a Jif cap on my vanity.

Don't recall how when we stopped
to put in three bucks of premium unleaded
Super America gave away a free loaf
of Wonder bread with every purchase.
Don't tell the committee
that holds the key to my future

we put the bread in the trunk
so we wouldn't be tempted
the loaf a gift to my mother
a morsel of evidence
to disprove our seemingly
wasted days.

But even from the trunk
we smelled it
through the Farm and Fleet spare
through the tan upholstered back seat
and the millions in lost coins
we smelled it.

Through the curls of our smoke
from the makeshift bong
a Mountain Dew can crushed in the middle
poked with a corsage needle
leftover from a homecoming dance
perhaps junior prom, we smelled it.

Parked beside a pond unthawed by spring
we pointed our bare toes north out the windows
and rolled Wonder bread balls
two Catholic school girls
whose souls bordered on lost
tossing crusts to the ganders.

Sacred Ground

It was an afternoon in the week before Easter.
The nuns at St. Clare Elementary had released
us to our families in the name of the resurrection.
That was when everything came down:
a barn and two houses were leveled at the edge of town
while surrounding winds took trees,

cars, a stray dog, and a wandering girl as temporary hostages.
When they were returned to earth,
they were changed–
they kept some of the twisting air inside of them
as if it were part of the ransom.

These were the trees that trembled
when there was no breeze,
their leaves swaying like slowly waving hands.
The cars had a whistle inside them
that no mechanic could explain.

The dog was a midnight dervish,
his mouth would not foam nor his eyes glaze,
but some nights when the prairie was still
but for the distant murmur of truck or train,
he would idle down the center line of Hovey Avenue
to writhe and undulate
to a sensual, frenzied music
we could not hear.

The girl floated down our street, a yellow leaf
suspended in the air, descending or ascending
but never quite touching the ground.
She rounded the corner of our lot
and thus had to have passed our shed
with its backplot of the burials of family pets.
She passed the makeshift graves,

and so our burial ground was consecrated by her passing,
our half-angel, half-girl,
the wind fluttering in her chest
with the singing deep in the earth
of what has lived and died,
or aloft, the spirits yet to descend,
hovering in the living air.

The Birthmother's Handbook

CARRIE ETTER

Choose another name for yourself, another city.
Prepare for the nuisance of the body,
a variegated allotment of pain and difficulty
that presages old age.

Rub your hands over your distending belly,
but not like a brass lamp, not like a crystal ball.
Rub as though you are polishing silverware,
its fine contours requiring slow work.

Listen to the doctor's requirements as a midwife.
Insist that no drugs be given during labor
so that pain might induce anger.
Curse the fetus from your womb.

Mark time's progress, the approaching end.
But above all, don't sing to him.
Don't name him.
Never let him become someone you could lose.

Numb

KARLA FRANK

You never even asked me if I wanted to know.
The village dog's head skewered
on a post outside your camp,
snakes coiling in your issue boots,
and the immense, dense humidity
wrapping its heavy weight around
your fragile ribs–pushing breath slowly
out of you.
Years of your life–what's yours
is not mine.
How, when I learned of these things
afterward, later, second hand, stranger-like,
how I was amazed,
and crushed.
Even the most human of feelings–
the anguish of returning to a country
with just as many enemies,
this time unarmed.
The helicopter war.
Your cells still imagine
the razor sharp burn of napalm,
your lungs the pungent smell of mustard gas.
Yet your memory fades
like the receding whoosh of copter blades,
disappearing into the thick mist
and sprawling canopy.

And with it goes my father.

This, the very beast that shaped you,
coddling you in heat and fear and filth.
You yourself are its slimy animal,
its beautiful, ugly enigma.
I am naive enough to want you back. To hope you'll
come float back down to me, and remind me
of the days we shared math lessons,
when I could still fit on your lap–
when the problems could be answered, solved.
In real time,
getting to know you is watching
dramatized cop shows, violence rehearsed,
bullies with a stupid soundtrack,
and being reminded of the time we connected–
fist to stomach, my air shooting out
of this chest you gave me
like a deflated balloon.
These moments of absolutely nothing,
then sudden, seething hate.

The Race

KARLA FRANK

I watch cat and mouse chases with grandma
in the big, green Ottoman
we two–with suspended breath–
hang on to the hope
of Jerry's wit winning again.

This is a time of peanut butter and jam
sandwiches–of life slapped between
two pieces of thin, white bread,
of hospital visits and bone marrow tests.

This is a Tom and Jerry reality
and the belief in the ridiculous–
the belief in Santa and the hope
for a full head of hair.

Cradled together in cool chartreuse,
we embrace true animation–
a world of bold, primary colors only.
No subtle shades.

Armed with finger sandwiches
and cool milk in filmy canning jars,
we brace ourselves for the future–
for the potential snap of the mouse's neck,
the crunch of bones in the cat's mouth.

Years later, these memories are pure energy
stored deep in my bones, the bond
that enables you to avoid the cat,
to turn all those corners unscathed and race to safety.

Our small bodies cozened together,
that green Ottoman held us like lovers every afternoon,
and I can still feel Grandma's slender fingers
clinging to me too tight.

I remember how her amazing strength
was so well hidden in that slight frame.

Rag Doll

MICHELE GONZALES

Coming up fast on a slow red light,
I realized that tug you feel,
that falling forward is the soul
pulling from your body, getting
stuck on your eyes, your nose,
your bellybutton–skin needles
stitching deep, pulling flesh threads
long through, holding it.
Once the car fell still,
I noticed Matt's indifferent hands
hard on the steering wheel's sides,
his thumb pumping to some slow pulse
on the radio I was too drunk
to recognize; he always drove fast,
stopped fast, no matter how much
I'd had to drink that night.
He was unaware of my eyes watching him
as he was of rain drops
sliding down the windshield.
Unaware of the soft cool you feel,
a tingle just under your chest and eyelids
when you fall whole again
back into your seat.

It's why you can take
a rag doll by the ankles,
fling her hard against the wall,
bend her back, her plug
bellybutton poking up
stuffing lumped
under her white,

stretched muslin.
Then lay her on the bed's edge,
red yarn hair reaching for the floor
her head sliding, following slow–
leave her there,
her round, black, shiny button eyes
keeping her face
something different than happy,
despite its pink stitched on smile.

China

MICHELE GONZALES

The loneliest sound
is just after shattered glass;
the silent pause
before the mop and the trash
that holds your eyes frozen
to china roses on the linoleum–broken.
In that sound, you imagine
your mother's fast cleaning hands
that catch moths and kill flies
with quick flat smacks–
how they slowed to touch
the painted porcelain on occasions only–slowed
to set over gentle lace
on the dining table, slowed to wash;
her rough, red, warm water thumbs
soothing bubbles over antique petals.
You remember her drying china
like a pink and thin memory
she was handling, fingers pulled
soft over every detail like
reading blind. You see
her carry it again
directly from the kitchen to the china-hutch,
ease the quiet doors over it,
then brush the dust from the cabinet glass–
push it away with her towel.

Everybody Loves the Devil
for Jordan Petrou Griffith

GAY BREWER

You find him under a harvest moon, in a hemp
basket fighting the river by your parents' farm.
You're wet to the thighs as you raise him
in his rotted blanket, pink-faced and bawling
with a tiny smile behind the suffering. *He's mine,*
you scream, *I deserve him, I don't care.*

When he pukes a little apple pudding on your
shoulder, it's a prophecy of better times.
When he squeezes his eyes and bellows damnation,
that means *I know everything tomorrow brings.*
You coo, *Little devil you're my darling,*
the boys at school don't know nothing about where
I've been. Daddy plays it tough and Mamma
waxes philosophic, and both raise hell
about your mystery father. But when baby spews
his stuff and dumps a stinking load of sin
they crumble like two who've refound the faith.

I remember them days, says Mamma. *Bastard's*
kind of cute, says Dada. Look how his eyes
glow and our angel girl shines like a new woman.
Everybody loves the devil. Everybody,
everybody. We watch him grow and grow and grow.

59

Mary

GAY BREWER

Mary's easy to make
so you have her in the morning
have her all day long
hot, the way she tastes best

Mary's full of blood and ice
spicy with dark secrets

She's the difference between lime
and lemon, a honeymoon
and reconciled for the children

She raises sleek green arms
like a mambo queen
to your salt and pepper misstep

When's the next holiday we
celebrate Mary coming, early?
What about today, darling–
right now, forever and always

A Crash of Rhinos

PAISLEY REKDAL

But it is illusion to think that there is anything fragile about this
life of the earth; surely this is the toughest membrane imaginable
in the universe, opaque to probability, impermeable to death.
We are the delicate part, transient and vulnerable as cilia. Nor
is it a new thing for man to invent an existence that he imagines
to be above the rest of life; this has been his most consistent
intellectual exertion down the millennia... (But) Man is
embedded in nature.
>   Lewis Thomas, *Lives of a cell*

What's your pet name? Collective noun?
What will Snookums do today? Your bedmate
pulls quarters magically from behind your ear, one
for each hour you've spent together. When he stops
there's fifty cents sliding into the sheets and his tongue
covering the pink cauliflower of your nipple. "Beautiful
defects," he whispers into your body. "Ah, Nature." Roll
>   away,
don't care when he calls you "Thumper." By noon you'll be
nose to nose anyway, a sloth of bears, snoozing
your way into this relationship.

Ah, Nature. You could tell him its startling fact
is not its defects but its sameness. A uniformity
suggestive of some single cell prototype, our Adam/ Eve
genome plucked, as scientists think, from the thread
of a lightning bolt. Darling, today you're more
than anonymous, one sexy blip among the thousand
couples grunting in each others arms; defined by Loving,

your action. Flying geese only recognized
by the form they make in the sky. And language reflects this.
A crash of rhinos, piece of asses. Stinkhead:
every thing comes in boring droves of hogs.

This is how you got here. Mid-morning he tallies your union
in terms of snakes, tarantulas, the evolutionary needs
of common flagellates, till you scorn science: it's primal urge
to pair like scared cows shoved ass to ass in circles
for defense. A clutch of penises. And what is love but fear?
That soft storm at your periphery, sudden hand
pushing you below surface? Thoughts, as you age or sicken,
sifted from consciousness like dusts of starlings: Love me,
little lamb. No one should die alone.

Sweetheart, all your friends are married.
Packs of teazles? Kerfs of panters? A multiplicity of spouses.
Today (ah, nature!) only two quarters protect you
from loneliness. It's out of your hands. The job
just didn't pan. Checks bounce, 2.a.m. is its own
worst child. A rout of wolves, cowardice of curs.
This is your last magic trick.
"Kumquat," he whispers. Lover. Loved one.
And the soul begs always, Leave me, leave me,
while the body says simply, Stay.

captain cook in tahiti discovers tattooing: an event that has subtle but important consequences for my parents and myself

PAISLEY REKDAL

July, 1769. King George Island. His first adventure
in diplomacy and all Cook can think about is food.
"I am of opinion that Victuals dress'd this way
are more juicy than by any of our methods, large fish
in particular, Bread fruit, Bananoes and Plantains Cook'd
like boiled Potatoes..." Food and tattoos. It's dusk.
In a glow of candlenuts his men sweat sullenly
over pineapple while the women rush off to stuff themselves
in private. That's when Cook notices. Those Zs toothed
to every knuckle and toe, crescents so blackly apparent, "so
                                  various
that both their quantity and situation seems to depend
entirely on the Humour of the individual." The Captain
                                  winces,
struggles to put more bread fruit away. Next morning
his first journalistic record is of the chieftain's arched
                                  buttocks,
tiairi's black curlicues smoking up each thigh as the man
drags in his breakfast.

"I'd work skin any day," says this month's *Slinging Ink*
                                  feature.
Skin Rag's blown up the tats so big a veil of sweat
gleams through like priming. "Though I admit
the gun buzz bothers me." On Saturdays my father
shaved behind closed doors. If I asked I could watch the flat
blade sucking over throat skin, then sit on the clean black
                                  couch
while mother vacuumed our stairwell. She hates the sould

of blades. "The Color they use is lamp black
prepared from the smook of a kind of Oily nutt," wrote Cook.
"The Instruments bone or shell struck into the skin so deep
every stroke is followed with a small quantity of blood."
Smokey Vaselines my thigh, watches skin
shrivel pink under his gun. Blood's pucker. A steady,
cupped rasp of bees. To take my mind off the pain I think
of anything: doughnuts, a wedding album. My father's face
and hair so pale beside his darker bride. I remember
for their anniversary I hung red *Fook* signs between doorways,
watched cellophane and ticker curl arterially
till the hours he drove home wakened deep moonrises,
set the night ink bleeding like an octopus over the city.

Why get one? Cook wondered, though the question wasn't
                                                   really
why but *when*. "As this is a painfull operation," he noted,
"it is perform'd but once in their life time, never
untill they are 12 or 14 years of age." Once is fine with me.
But "If I had bare white skin again," says Smokey's girl,
                                                   Karleen,
"I'd start getting those tattoos." My mother won't
give blood, get shots or share combs, calls ear piercing
barbaric. A cultural tick, she argues. The mark
of the lower classes. After a lunch of plantains Cook limps
beachward to watch his sailors cavort with local girls, whose
                                                   lower
faces, ink-starred, collapse in muddy smiles. Cook knows
what lives abroad can't work at home. He gives them time.
And there's sympathy for them, as when he notes the sailors'
longings muffled behind bathhouses and canoes, the men and
                                                   women

who "look upon it as a freedom from which they value
                                                    themselves"
wrestling into each other; proteans evolving second forms.
After a month he sees even his starchiest officers work nude.
And on their bare backs: black arches. Flat, elliptical moons.

I figure I can hide it; just never change clothes when she's
                                                    around.
"This'll Last Longer Than Your Marriage!" *Tat-Way*'s slogan
                                                    boasts
beside its graphic: a knife plunged into a bleeding cupcake.
Paris, 1968. Mother sends her telegram announcing the
                                                    wedding
two days after New Year's. "I'm sorry," it says.
"But I wanted to." No, from my experience nothing's as
                                                    foreign
to her as apology. And by this time the Kans must have
                                                    expected it;
not one child yet married Chinese. But white?
No gifts shuttle via mail, no congratulations are exchanged.
Most don't know to what depth artists repeatedly place the
                                                    pigment,
nor where it rests–whether in corium, melanin layer, bottom
of the dermis, the papillae. Fact is, the tattoo's permanence
is due to the thin cyst layered beneath pigment, the failing of
                                                    skin
to eject its foreign elements. "There is no denying the high
sexual significance of tattooing," writes Phil Andros.
Which might explain my mother's furtive examination
of my dresser drawers when she discovers the cache of tattoo
                                                    mags,
the way she tries surprising me in the shower when visiting
by lurking behind the bathroom door.

"This just expresses the crazy side of me," says Carleen,
flexing her abs. "Since we're both smokers, a Zippo
seemed appropriate." Smokey's thin blade digs shamelessly
towards my pelvis. I speculate on my parent's possible
                                                    reactions;
recall Stainsby writing behind Cook's back: "Myself,
and some others of our company, underwent the operation
and had our arms marked." No one knows what happened to
                                                    him.
He might have been beheaded in the later raid. Or he made it
back to England, reluctantly, where his wife,
(his mistress, the young male lover perhaps?) recoiled at sight
of flesh pebbled blackly. But then she too became
                                                    accustomed
enough that the sight of his lined chest made palms sweat
with longing. Like lying in the arms of savages, being
                                                    devoured
by geometry... Which might have been the way
my mother expressed her new husband's body to herself, their
                                                    uncharted
skins marbled by the weak Paris street lights coming off the
                                                    sill.
"We're never coming back," she writes. Though they do,
hand-in-hand, resigned to three months pregnancy.
"One little tat," says Carleen. "That's all it took for me."

"... fathom water an owsey bottom, the shore of bay a sandy
                                                    beach..."
Imagine the sight of new land, islands like stockings in a tub
                                                    of water.
My father and mother step down from their respective
trains and scan La Gare Nord in its grainy fog, the smell of
                                                    dogs
and coffee wafting towards them from the Metro. Vendors
yawn their customers aside; two Algerians hurry into a café.

"They are of various colours, nay some of the women
are almost as fair as Europeans..." mused Cook
upon first meeting the Tahitians. Which thought occurred
to my father, seeing her six years after school's passage
and a stint in the army. The autumn, like her hair, smelled of
                                                                                    rain.
"With tattoos you never have to go cruising
the bars and baths, looking for beauty..." (*Skin Rag*)
No indeed, it follows you. Sun springs hotly
from its cloud and the stationary trains wait like capped
                                                                                    needles.
Smokey, done, hands me cellophane. My parents-to-be
(sensing this? sensing me?) stop in their tracks blinded
by this sight of each other. *And before* this? Round the bend
of bay Cook's men spy the beach, the chieftain and his
                                                                                    tattooed
daughters waiting. Slowly his sailors lower their oars.
Then cover their eyes in greeting.

Body Habits

Oprah is occupied today with a string of women
who've recorded their husbands' snores,
who've taken the last they can take
of earplugs, earphones, heads tucked under pillows
before early morning moves to the couch.
Lacking recognition, support,
understanding of their true heroics,
they've put up with all
they could reasonable endure.
So they've set the cassettes,
planned ahead for the cameras,
the heat of the lights,
as if they will finally resolve something important,

as if those recorded could ever sound familiar to themselves
and everyone should catch their bodies
at the things they do on their own.
These women want responsibility made clear,
established through the whole of a marriage, job,
habit of sitting daily at the same table
where a family grimaces over the way the toddler smacks his
cereal loudly,
mouth opening wide with each bite,
the Dad makes tiny burps between gulps of coffee,
and the Mom nervously twists crumbs
from her toast into her hair.

On stage, is a woman who sleeps in a near fetal arch,
butt stretched so far across the bed
there is no room for anyone's habits
to blend into her turns and tosses.
Her husband jokes that it is impossible
to stay in the same building when she sleeps,
let alone the same mattress.

She is told constantly, *scoot over, scoot over,*
keep the covers straight, as if she could summon
more command in dreams than awake,
than she ever did as a child
when people said *look at me, look at me*
while she memorized patterns of ceilings–
how gold flecks and brown water spots
blurred into circular sorry resentments
as her knuckles pressed painfully together,
her chin quivered softly through the revelation
of some vague incomprehensible guilt
over hurting her brother,
letting too much homework slip by.
On stage, is another woman who would understand,
who would like to make a place for herself
and stay in it, would like to
settle spoon fashion through the night
with no restless puttering from room to room,
but the thought of learning how
makes her lips draw together like her mother's
when they cannot be opened without anger,
and she knows this much– the man
who asks it of her snores without apology
like the other talk show examples
who've found themselves married to women
who toss, sigh, fart, cough, unendingly,
unrecorded, in the night.

1-70: Reconstruction Blues

NATHANIEL PERRINE

Twenty miles west of Ogden, Kansas,
the slowest rain begins to fall,
spitting in the face of my windshield, in between the
abandoned wooden tracks and silos that silently decay into
the gut of our heartland I sit behind my brights, sticking to
a superman 40-hour diet of stale gas station coffee,
                                                    Zing-Zongs,
and a half-ounce of smoke, all in attempt to keep
my troubled mind in a state of blissful ecstacy, *not gonna
get the best of me, no sir.*

Clicking the wipers by hand, on/off, on/off
I hit Missouri, now I know
this drizzle's not gonna quit, not until
it slams into the rolling Appalachians of West Virginia and
Pennsylvania, where this spitting drizzle will unleash a
blanketing rain, quickly filling the rust-belt valley towns like
swimming pools in the spring.

Behind me lay the coastal headlands of Australia, the quiet
sunbaked coves of Southern California and the girl with the
high voice I met on the beach that I swore I'd marry.
The unfolding waves
crash, chasing at my rear tires. In front of me, the soft hills
of Pennsylvania, the open arms of my recently divorced
mother, my
emotionally crippled brother and this eternal rain, of course,
keeping
my wheels afloat. The beautiful foreshadowing of my life
                                                    slapping me in the
face, once again.

70

I wake from a numbing nap on the edge of Illinois,
grey and damp
with traffic so intense it becomes a game
—the caffeined stoner versus corporate
America on Prozac, I take the lead,
hopping lanes past construction bottlenecks and
tireless roadworkers who sit
on the median smoking. Meanwhile
the commuters have taken the backseat,
smiling and watching the workers
in the rain; America the beautiful,
land of enchantment, land of orange
cones and yellow pills. I giggle in the rain, too.

Nighttime settles through Ohio, smoke from the pipe fills me
painfully tickling the apex of my lungs.
I play Joni Mitchell and the rain opens
up over the bridge to Wheeling, West Virginia,
giving the river a
copper glow, the breakdown
is coming. I hear my mother at 28, singing Joni's
California tune in the kitchen, her voice rises up the walls
raising the ceiling from its eaves,
the sun slips in the sliding glass door
through the hanging spider plants,
over the pine wood floors and warms my face
while I eat my pancakes. The Pennsylvania Turnpike sign
reflects over my lap and face,
I pee in a bottle to save time.

The Turnpike off-ramp rounds east, around and around
to the last light flashing red, my arm and eyeballs shake with
the hum of the highway. Side streets and strip malls
go by without a blink,
past the farmer's market, past the deli.
Past the corner bus-stop where I
beat-up Jimmy Mullens, who always picked
on my brother but really I just
didn't like the way he looked.
He had a scowl that would shatter cheval mirrors.

My mother hears the door and I hear the stairs
from the couch. I can feel her leaning
over me from the back of the sectional
but I pretend to be asleep
like I did when I was a boy, not ready to talk.
In the flat light of morning,
My brother sits at my feet, chewing his toast loudly,
taunting me, He asks how
long I will stay this time, and I want to tell him everything.
I tell him
only 'til the clouds give way,
He gives me a funny look,
I just lay there and smile.

For Sale: Fictional Characters. Cheap.

MEISHA ROSENBERG

A real person, paying to become fictional. It seems tainted, like prostitution; as though one should only become fictional through an act of love. When I first learned of someone becoming fictional like this, I did not want to believe it; it seemed to herald disaster. I thought of a quotation, attributed to writing on a tablet dating back to 2800 B.C. and found near Babylon: "The world must be coming to an end. Children no longer obey their parents and every man wants to write a book." A modern-day tablet might say: "The world must be coming to an end. Children no longer obey their parents, and everybody wants to be a character in a book." The problem with everyone wanting to write a book is that you would have no readers left, no one left to appreciate literature other than their own. The problem with everyone wanting to be a character is that we will have no readers and no writers. If our society values only actors, agents, characters–those who do– we will have no room for the people who observe and make sense of what we do.

Michael is one of the black sheep in my family. At a family gathering in 1994 he said "You're a writer–I should tell you this: I'm famous, you know. I'm in a book." The rest of our conversation went something like this:

"You're famous? Do tell."

Michael said, "I was at an auction and I won the prize of being in Stephen King's latest book, *Insomnia*."

"What?"

"I'm in *Insomnia*. I'm famous."

"Are you yourself? Who are you?" I stammered.

"No, not exactly. But I am a character."

"You've got to be kidding. Who? A main character?"

"Unfortunately I'm not a main character. I'm Connie Chung's cameraman."

I asked Michael to reiterate what he had told me three more times. I said, "Michael, you know you could have come to me any time, and I would have written about you, for free."

I'm related to a fictional character. Not only that: he's Connie Chung's cameraman. It would be nice to think of Michael's story as an isolated, self-contained event having no implications for the world we live in. His appearance in fiction is, in one sense, a freak event, an aberration. But freak events of a certain nature are becoming more common in the world of literature today, and Michael's story reveals some of the disturbing undercurrents of a trend. I found the book in a bookstore and sat down to conduct an examination. *Insomnia* resembles a brick, in design, in bulk, and in its effect on the human head. I later learned that *Insomnia* is one of King's thinner works. Another of his books, oddly enough entitled *Thinner*, totals a fat healthy 1135 pages. *Insomnia* is a paltry 787 pages.

The plot of King's *Insomnia,* like many of his other plots, is about a disenfranchised member of society: an old man who lives in Derry, Maine. Ralph Roberts, newly widowed, can't sleep at night, and he starts seeing auras and "little bald doctors" who resemble the space aliens commonly depicted in tabloids. Ralph and his girlfriend, Lois, are on a mission ordained from above to rescue Derry from "The Random." This involves sucking the aural life-forces out of others (nobody gets hurt from this, though) and saving an abortion-rights activist from a rabid pro-lifer. Following are excerpts from the text of my cousin's cameo appearance as a fictional character. In total he is given six less-than-spectacular mentions.

"Connie Chung walked out from beneath the canopy with a bearded, handsome cameraman–MICHAEL ROSENBERG the tag on his CBS jacket said–and then raised her small hands in a framing gesture, showing him how she wanted him to

74

shoot the bed sheet banner hanging down from the canopy. Rosenberg nodded. Chung's face was pale and solemn, and at one point during her conversation with the bearded cameraman, Ralph saw her pause and raise a hand uncertainly to her temple, as if she had lost her train of thought or perhaps felt faint..." (593).

"'Stick around, lady,' Michael Rosenberg called. 'You'll see all kinds of wildlife here tonight.' There was some desultory, almost forced laughter, and then they turned back to their task'" (595).

"The auras of the news people were like the small but brightly colored Japanese lanterns glowing bravely in a vast, gloomy cavern. Now a tight beam of violet light speared out from one of them–from Michael Rosenberg. Connie Chung's bearded cameraman, in fact. It divided in two an inch or so in front of Lois's face. The upper branch divided in two again and slipped into her nostrils; the lower branch went between her parted lips and into her mouth" (594).

The bulk of these quotations is simply Michael's name, sometimes in capital letters, repeated. Also repeated are the words "handsome" and "bearded." In reality my cousin Michael is bearded–"handsome," however, is not a word even Michael uses to describe himself. Michael's "character" in *Insomnia*–more of an extra than a character–has no relation to Michael as a person, except the letters in his name. Michael does not get to save Derry from bald doctors; he does not get to see auras or even commit fictional acts of depravity. Michael's one comment is a cliche` ("You'll get to see all kinds of wildlife here tonight.") All signs of personality vanish from Michael. Even his aura gets ripped off when Lois sucks it out of him.

What is the running price of fictionality these days? I called my cousin and he agreed to talk with me. At the Fantasy Auction on March 4, 1991, Michael won the prize of appearing as a fictional character in King's next novel. At $12,000, Michael was the highest bidder. The proceeds of the benefit went to the Manhattan Center for Living, a charity organization helping homeless people and runaways.

Michael's appearance in fiction is a small part of a growing phenomenon. This phenomenon has many manifestations, in film, in books, in real life, on television. Some of its manifestations are harmless, some annoying, some dangerous and disturbing. For convenience, and in keeping with King's penchant for matters of re- and incarnation, let's call the phenomenon "fictional incarnation." Fictional incarnation is the act by which a real person is made a fictional character. There is an important difference between fictional incarnation and the reference to a real person in a work of fiction: fictional incarnation has to occur either through a purchase or donation, but in any case through a monetary exchange. The importance of this difference will become apparent later on.

As long as thrill seekers aren't cheated, and as long as they keep it in perspective, fictional incarnation can be harmless. It can be beneficial to both sides of the transaction. For example, the March 18-19 edition of the *International Herald Tribune* reported in 1995 that "An advertisement that recently appeared in *The Times* and other national newspapers offered 'Your Chance to Play a Part in British Film History' and meant it literally: Buying one share in the production at a cost of 1,000 pounds (about $1,600) entitles the purchaser to appear as an extra in what is described as 'the powerful story of Scotland's great warrior king.'" Kirk Carruthers, a 35-year-old producer, originally dreamed up this scheme for a Scottish epic film about Bonnie Prince Charlie called "Chasing the Deer," which opened in 1994 and drew 284 small investors. Mary Blume, author of the article, wonders "Would a big investor have a chance at a juicy speaking role instead of just carrying a bucket or holding a spear? 'Probably not,' Carruthers said though some extras in "Chasing the Deer" fought on both sides of the battle and one man died twice."

Carruthers needed to raise money in order to produce his films, which, so far, are not blockbusters. In the absence of funding for artistic ventures, fictional incarnation may well be a useful tool. Still, one can't help but notice the desperation that fuels this kind of entrepreneurial gambit, both on the side of the characters/shareholders, and on the side of the artists and producers trying to come up with new ways to fund art. One has to wonder how long Carruthers' venture and similar ventures will remain nobly in the service of an impoverished art: he planned to make his next film, also with appearances offered to investors, appeal to a more mainstream audience.

The most mainstream example of this trend occurred in 1995 with a promotional stunt by Showtime. Called the Showtime Big Break Sweepstakes, it was a "no-purchase necessary" lottery, and if your ticket was the winner, Showtime agreed (not without some legal disclaimers) to give you a "walk-on (non-speaking) role in a Showtime original production." The non-speaking element of these forays into fictionality points to the draw: the temptation of becoming fictional is not about speaking, but rather just about being fictional–a state which seems to allow the potential "winners" of these stunts a kind of privileged silence. Like in my cousin Michael's case, these fictional characters are not about communication, but rather are about fantasy, escapism, distance. The tickets said that the Showtime drawing would be judged by "Marden-Kane, an independent judging organization," and the entry tickets asked nothing more than your name and address. An advertisement for this "big break," shown during the previews of movies, flashed tantalizing scenes of movie stars before viewers' eyes, making it seem like you could be one of them.

We have seen two examples of fictional incarnation in the movies. To what extent has this caught on in books? To my knowledge there have been at least two examples of my cousin Michael's particular kind of fictional incarnation, in which, due to a donation, a previously unknown person appears as a character in a novel. Carolyn Banks is a mystery writer who lives in Austin, Texas, and belongs to the Central Texas Dressage Society, an organization that holds an annual auction. Banks told me in 1994 that "a few years ago they had an auction and I didn't have anything to contribute, so I offered a character." Usually the club auctions horse riding equipment and proceeds go towards things like free riding clinics with top name instructors. "They fought it out, and then Cathy Schwetman [also a member of the Dressage Society] won. Then she wanted to be a villain. So she became Katerina Schwetman." The novel, *Death by Dressage*, was the first in a series. In the end Schwetman "dies a wretched death," and she and her family were thoroughly pleased with the results. Schwetman even signed at an autograph party.

Similar to Banks's donation was that of mystery writer J. A. Jance: in the author's note to her J. P. Beaumont mystery *Lying in Wait*, published in 1994, we read, "I want to acknowledge the wonderful folks who made generous donations to local charities in order to be part of this story. As my mother would say, 'Whoever you are, you know who you are.'" Despite all the down-home altruism here, one has to wonder why fiction, perhaps no longer salvation in itself, has become a vehicle for charity.

Unlike Michael and our examples in film, Jance and Banks donated characters not to make a profit or to fund their writing, but to fund charities of various kinds. Schwetman influenced the nature of her character: she was a full character, not just an extra. Carolyn Banks and J. A. Jance provide us with the most human examples of fictional incarnation. Carolyn Banks, unlike King and Carruthers, did not just sell her character to anyone who could afford the highest price; she auctioned it to someone she knew.

Fabio is perhaps the most well-known example of fictional incarnation, and he has no end other than to make a killing. Fabio has transformed himself into hundreds of fictional characters, through association with his photo on romance novel covers. He is both fictional character, and fictional author: he hires others to write the books for which he supplies the plot. Fictional authorship is not uncommon, by the way; V. C. Andrews's latest works of fiction carry a statement claiming that, even though she is dead, her works continue to be written (almost from beyond the grave, as it were) by "a carefully selected writer." Fabio, in addition to being a fictional author, now has his own TV show, "Acapuleo H.E.A.T.," and his own album, "Fabio After Dark," with songs sung by other people. Fabio has dual citizenship in the real world and in the world of romances, and consequently he enjoys elevated status in both. And becoming fictional is not just for Fabio anymore.

Take the shrewdest elements of Fabio, mix them with Carolyn Banks' donation of a character to someone who was allowed to participate actively in the creation of her persona, and throw in Carruthers' idea of characters being shareholders, and you've got a great book marketing scheme. Some day perhaps everyone will have the opportunity to become a character by paying publishers or writers. Hey buddy–you want to be a character in my story? Pay me $5,000. You can be anyone–thin, beautiful, handsome, rich. Advertisements in the back of magazines would read "For Sale: Fictional characters. Cheap." The publishing industry could sell characters as a way to make up for the revenue they are losing in the face of competition from the video and computer industries.

Publishers and writers could sell characters not only to privately bidding individuals, but to companies; perhaps liquor companies. Does that sound too far-fetched? It's not in 1997, now that we have what Janny Scott calls in her *New York Times* article of March 10, 1997, "the literary liquor-company-sponsored soir`ee." In this hybrid event, a liquor company (Johnnie Walker and Macallan among them) tries to get some of the glamour of writers to rub off on their product by holding a reading with free dinner and drinks. The audience usually consists of a targeted section of a magazine's readership, often youngish people who marketers think could be trend setters; publications that have participated include *Harper's Magazine* and *Granta*. One writer who read at one of these events, Thomas Beller, complained that the liquor company representatives shoved a glass of their scotch in his hands before trying to take his picture. I was myself recently invited to a "Spirited Celebration of the Written Word" by *Harper's Magazine* and the Macallan Single Highland Malt Scotch Whiskey company. It was a benefit for the Freedom-to-Write committee of PEN, with a reading by John Irving. As a conscientious objector, I did not attend: when high-marketing concepts get this close to the literary life, I am wary. How far off are we from liquor endorsements in fiction itself: "And then Celia lifted a glass of Macallan Single Highland Malt Scotch Whiskey to her lips, and sighed that her husband was so far away...".

These kinds of benefits and marketing schemes could turn into a frightening world with wealthy readers controlling literary content, characters who are sold like slaves, and writers who are themselves slaves to profit. But this "demise of literature" scenario is unlikely, as are most 'demise of literature scenarios. Even if fictional incarnation took off as a marketing concept, publishing wouldn't be any worse off than it is. Publishing is already a profit-driven industry dependent on its most popular books, and these books are exactly books like *Insomnia* and Fabio's romances. Literature does not face a dramatic, apocalyptic end, but rather a wearing away, a blurring of values that has been going on for quite a while.

Michael's appearance in fiction is difficult to judge morally, not only because it is blended with a charity, but also because it is less an appearance and more of a disappearance. Unlike Fabio, Michael made no profit. Unlike Catherine

Schwetman, he had no contact with the author nor impact on his character. Unlike the British film-maker and his shareholders, Michael was not part of an exciting new trend in movie-marketing. Michael gets lost in the enormous text of *Insomnia* and in its staggering statistics. Just in terms of sheer mass marketing effort, *Insomnia* is impressive. Viking spent one million dollars on marketing alone. The 1994 Viking Penguin catalog describes the "Pre-publication advertising" as a "stealth campaign." "One month before publication, we'll infiltrate every type of media–TV, newspapers, magazines, transit, even online services. All we'll say is: INSOMNIA. IT LOOMS. We'll say it over and over, in as many ways possible, in as many places as possible. We'll get the buzz going...enticing King's fans as well as a new generation of readers."

The point of this marketing statement was not really to "infiltrate" the media, but rather to create a mood around King's works. Viking actively encourages paranoia in King's readership. (It's a completely coincidental but ironic fulfillment of Viking's threatening marketing statement that King got himself an honest-to-goodness stalker, who followed him to readings and was convinced up until his arrest in the winter of 1994 that King was John Lennon's murderer.) King's works inspire disassociation, and Viking's marketing statement mirrors this state of mind. It is this disassociation which characterizes Michael's appearance in the text of *Insomnia*. This quality differentiates Michael's fictional incarnation from the other examples of fictional incarnation we have mentioned and from a long history of real people appearing in fictional works.

One of the oldest examples of actual people appearing in fiction and art is patronage, with its explicit financial relationship between patron and artist. Jacobean English literature is filled with references and dedications in poetry and drama to patrons, countesses, sirs, queens and kings, who were lining the writer's purse. Ben Jonson dedicates this 1616

81

poem to one of his patroness, Lucy, Countess of Bedford: "Lucy, you brightness of our sphere, who are! Life of the Muses' day, their morning star!" In another version of a Jonson poem to Lucy, her name, like Michael's, is capitalized: "You, and that other starre, that purest light!/ Of all LUCINA'S traine; LUCY the bright!/ Then which, a nobler heaven it selfe knowes not..."

But in comparing relationships of historical literary patronage to Michael's transaction with King–who would be the patron? In one sense Michael played the traditional role of patron since he gave money in order to be incorporated into a work of art. But his place in the book is trivial. Also, both Michael and King are rich, and Michael didn't give anything directly to King. King himself is in a position to be patron to others. Also unlike the past, Michael is utterly disconnected in any human way from King's writing. Further evidence of the strange alienation hovering over Michael and King's transaction is that the Manhattan Center for Living is no longer operating under that name, and no one in Michael's or King's service could locate the person who came up with the "Fantasy Auction" idea to begin with.

All ties, except for those few paragraphs in the book, have been cut. The Fantasy Auction–"fantasy" in more ways than one–took place at Sotheby's, but Michael never even went there. He telephoned his bids in to a representative. Michael and Stephen King have never met. Michael and King are a perfect match, patron and writer disassociated within a context of superficial materialism. Michael said about reading *Insomnia*, "I got sidetracked and only read the first 300 pages. My friend got through it and told me where I was. Every time I look at the book on my bookcase, I get a chuckle out of it. I think maybe in 30 or 40 years someone might look at it and chuckle." What does it mean that Michael, a fictional character, cannot read through the book in which he appears? Besides the fact that it does not speak well for King's writing, it does not bode well for the state of literature or for the relationship between fiction and life.

In order to understand further how Michael and King deviate, we need to know what they deviate from–in other words, what is the relationship between life and fiction in contemporary art as we understand it? All writers work in part by forging their own realities into fiction. They declare their own lives to be fictional, taking from the reality of their lives in order to create something more, something of artistic worth. It can feel like a theft. But this turning of the dross of reality into fictional gold is a far cry from Michael's real gold being turned into Stephen King's fictional dross. King and Michael have reversed the traditional creative process.

Our society's hunger for a fake reality has gotten out of hand, becoming a commodity itself that competes with the increasingly market-controlled realm of fiction. This has allowed a reversal in the process by which reality is usually transformed into truth, that is, into the transcendent truth of art. With *I Want To Tell You* by OJ Simpson, and *Real Stories of the Highway Patrol*, reality has become a cash crop. King's fiction has more in common with the hyper-reality of *Real Stories of the Highway Patrol* than it does with great fiction because King trades on an inflated reality and not on truth.

What distinguishes a serious work of art from the rest has something to do with truth, and also something to do with fear. King made a comment in an interview that betrays his relationship to fear: "I've always believed that if you think the very worst, then, no matter how bad things get (and in my heart I've always been convinced that they can get pretty bad), they'll never get as bad as that. If you write a novel where the bogeyman gets somebody else's children, maybe they'll never get your own children." King here admits he does not write out of his own suffering. Rather, by writing about "fear," and fictionalizing "the very worst" he provides an experience for his readers of simulated terror from which they can exit snug in the contentment of their own protected realities. Like the

83

trailer for the movie *Breakdown*–"What if the worst happened?" –King's books appeal to our desire to return to a static and safe present.

King writes by preying on the fears and insecurities of others in order to stave off his own fear of death. Similarly, Ralph, his main character in *Insomnia*, stays young by sucking the life auras out of others. Ralph and King are similar, and both in turn are like Michael. Michael said that, before the auction, he was not particularly a Stephen King fan. "His books give me nightmares, [but] it appealed to me. Unlike buying some piece of sports memorabilia or Judy Garland's shoes from the *Wizard of Oz*, with this you're almost immortal. It's almost immortality because the books of a writer as successful as King stay around forever and sometimes are movies." Michael is unable to face his own mortality. Like Dorian Gray, Michael, King, and Ralph try to keep suffering and mortality at bay, not by engaging it with words, but by keeping it back with materiality, whether with a painting, with a megalomaniac dream of aura-sucking, or with a physical fortress of paper.

The difference between Dorian Gray and Michael/King/Ralph is that Dorian Gray had a true artist watching over him: Oscar Wilde. Although Dorian Gray may not have admitted to his moral decay, Oscar Wilde knew, and his message within his book is that the artist's vision shows the truth, as horrible and unreal as it may seem.

King as an author hides as soon as the messiness of this truth threatens to appear. This is exemplified by something I learned later on in my investigations. Neither Michael nor King's spokespeople gave me, at first, the complete picture. King originally had requested a brief autobiography and photo of Michael. Michael complied, but "apparently after seeing my face and reading my biography they couldn't do much with it. Not that I've done much with it, either." That was what Michael said. It is only partly true. The other side of the story came eventually from a spokesperson in King's office, who reported that Michael initially intended to give his character to his wife. Then they got a divorce. It was such a negative experience for King to deal with the fallout from this situation that, according to his spokesperson; he swears he will never donate a character again.

This unfortunate personal event in Michael's life became tangled up with his appearance in fiction. The way King dealt with this was to not deal with it: to gloss over Michael's problems, put him in *Insomnia* but not as himself, and to swear to never donate a character again. What King did with Michael is exactly what he does with his other characters. King is unable to deal with an unfortunately complicated reality. And aren't we all unable to an extent? Can't we see ourselves in him? Reading his books, instead of making me dislike him, made me understand where he fails. His penchant for evading a problem that he nobly sets out to tackle explains partly what's so appealing about him. King would make a much better character than he does a writer. He sets impossible tasks for himself, like trying to explain and figure out all contemporary phenomena all at once in one novel, from abortion debates to auras to alien sightings and old age. He puts all these things together, and it is so important to him to provide us with some explanation, some master conspiracy for our problems. But all he does is put these troubling phenomena together in a blender and press puree. Or he starts out, like in *Insomnia*, with a sincere problem or issue–like old age–and then proceeds to run as fast as he can, weaving in circles around it, coming up with outlandish fantasies to evade it.

But there is still hope for Michael. Perhaps there is something better for Michael than immortality. Michael's reality is stranger than fiction. I am never really sure what he does in life. Mostly he is professionally rich. Michael always has a new gadget–he calls it his "state-of-the-art"–like a giant eraser or a movie-screen-sized television in his apartment. I think he has been excruciatingly lonely. It would be a

85

fascinating story, the tale of Michael's true life. Fiction–not of the *Insomnia* variety–might be the lie that is the only thing flexible enough to tell Michael's strange truth. I'd like to go back for a moment to the party where I first saw him after many years. He kind of stumbled into the room, and moved around from table to buffet, restlessly looking for some cranny or seat that is his, not finding one. He shuffles when he walks, and talks out of the corner of his mouth, sarcastically mumbling about himself in order to prevent anyone else from doing so. He has shifty eyes. Watching him, one can see him fluctuate between being a suspicious, leering character, and being a small, harmless boy.

Michael has a secretary and a lawyer. Michael's lawyer also has a lawyer. I know this because the lawyers both had to be consulted before Michael would consent to talk with me about his appearance in *Insomnia*. Michael has an alarm system hooked up to his house that is so sensitive, storms and heavy sheets of rain will set it off. Michael traveled to several Asian countries this winter, to visit a scientist friend of his who apparently has come up with a new theory of the creation of life.

Once, when I was fifteen and staying with my mother at Michael's New York apartment, he came home late at night. It was the last night of our stay in the city. Michael was drunk, yet he remembered to give me a present of perfume. He slurred my name and handed me a wrapped box. The next day, he asked me several times if he had remembered to give me my present. I never forgot this act of kindness, in the midst of his failure. This is material King could have used, if he bothered to know it. It is rich with questions unanswered, hints, and sadnesses.

The Father, Unblinking

BRIAN EVENSON

He had that day found his daughter dead from what must have been the fever, her swollen eyes stretching her lids open. The day had been a bright day, without clouds. He had found his daughter facedown in the sun-thick mosquito-spattered mud, by the back corner, where the dark paint had started taking air underneath and was flaking off the house now and falling apart at a touch like burnt turkey skin. He squatted over her and turned her up, and she came free with a sucking, the air coming out of her in a sigh, blowing bubbles of mud on her lips. He smeared away the mud from around her mouth. He worked at bending the body straight until the muck on her face dried ashy, then cracked.

He slapped mosquitos dead on her. He picked her up, folded her best he could, and carried her across the yard. He ducked under the window, hurried past the worn back stoop with the door at the top of it. He kicked hens and chicks out of the way, booting loose turbid clouds of pinfeathers. Hooking the barn door with his boot, he hop-skipped back until it was open wide enough to let his foot free and for him to shoulder himself and his girl in. It was quiet inside, and dark except for the shafts of light from the roof traps, four long pillars of bright dust descending to the scatterings of hay below.

He went to the far wall and ran his eyes over the hooks and what hung there: shears, axe, hatchet, hacksaw, handsaw, hand-rake, horse-rake, pitchfork, hoe. He stood staring, running his eyes over them again from the beginning. He looked over each shoulder in turn, turned in a slow circle in the half-dark of the barn, and walked jaggedly around the barn, kicking apart the damp clumps of hay that coated his boots in a yellow mold.

Moving hay in loads across the uneven dirt with his boots, he dragged some together in a pile at the far wall and put her atop the pile. He brushed the dirt off the dress, pulled the socks up past the calves again, loosened the buckles of the blunt-ended shoes. He scooped up an armload of hay and dumped it on top of her.

He scraped the soles of his boots on the edge of the stoop. He stamped a few times, pulled the screen open, went in.

She was cutting venison into thin strips. "Your shoes good?" she said.

"Yes," he said. "Boots," he said.

"Better be," she said, and turned in a squint toward him, red hands and all.

He held on to the end of the counter and lifted first one foot, then the other.

"Pass," she said, and went back to cutting.

"Seen my spade?" he said. "The long-handled job?"

"What for?" she said. "What do I want with it?" she said. "You seen it or not?" he said.

"You lent it out to Quade," she said. "Your mind's a blunt one today."

"I reckon it is not," he said. "Quade, is it?"

"Heard me, or did you?" she said.

He saw her shoulder blades shiver beneath the dress with each blow. He did not say a thing.

"You seen your little lullaby?" she said as he pushed open the screen.

He stopped.

"I haent seen her," he said.

"You tell her get her butt in here, you see her," she said.

"I haent seen her," he said. He pushed out onto the stoop, letting the screen clap to. "You know where I'm off," he said, loud.

"I know where," she called.

He went into the barn, to the far wall, and took down the hoe. Uncovering the girl's face, he looked at her, then covered her quickly over again. He went out with the hoe in his hands. Drawing the doors shut, he jammed the handle of the hoe through where the rings lined. Grunting, he shook the doors, pulled on their handles.

   He set off down the path, walking on the mounded sides instead of down in the ruts. The day was a bright day. Without clouds. The mud in the low spots was drying up, going white and hard. He walked the sunlit half-mile downslope to Quade's fence. There were ants aswarm, darkening the knotty rails. Jumping up, he grabbed the old oak limb. He swung a time or two and then heel-smashed the gate, shaking off hordes of ants, leaving the gate ashiver. He took a few more swings to make his body really go, and then flung himself over to the other side.

"Hey, Quade," he said, from the door.

Quade looked up from the box he was nailing, his half–gaunt face red and stringy, lumpy as the flesh of an old rabbit slaughtered too late.

"Bet I know what you are after," said Quade.

"Bet you do," the man said.

Quade spat nails into the box, dropped his hammer on the dirt. He rubbed the sweat off his neck, undid his bags to let them slide off his waist down to the floor. He went to a corner which sprouted handles. Messing about for a bit, he pulled forth an axe from the angry snarl.

"That mine?" said the man.

"Isn't it?" said Quade.

"Hell," said the man, spitting. "I come for the spade."
Quade squinted, looked at the axe. "Well, whose the hell is
this?" he said.

The man shrugged.

Quade went back to the snarl, fished around, poked his
way through it, drew out tool after tool, leaning them in a row.
His hands hanging loose, he stood staring at the row of
handles stacked stiff against the mold-blistered wall.

"Well, I'll be damned if I know where it got to," he said.

"Got to have it today," said the man.

"What you need it for?" said Quade.

"Digging," said the man.

"Digging what?" said Quade.

"Just digging," said the man.

Quade shook his head and went out. The man scavenged
loose a quarter sheet of plywood from underfoot, threw it on
top of the box, and eased his full weight down upon it. The
wood had been ripped ragged on one end, leaving a furry
edge. Bending down, he picked up the hammer, hefted it, let
it fall onto the dirt. He stared at his big, empty hands. On the
inside of one of his thumbs was a shiny gray smear.

Quade came back in, shovel in hand. He stopped moving
at the sight of the man.

"Can't say it is good luck to be sitting on that," said
Quade, "even with the plywood between."

"It don't matter, Quade," said the man. "It really don't."
Quade shrugged. The man took his time to stand up and reach
for the shovel.

"How's the wife?" said Quade.

"Good," said the man, taking.

"The girl," said Quade.

"Sick," said the man.

"You take care of those two," said Quade.

"You got it," said the man, walking out the door.

Opening the latch with his shovel blade, he let the ant-
ridden gate swing his way. He went through, on the other side

turning the shovel scoop-down and reaching back over the gate with it, dragging it back, pulling the gate closed. He smashed a couple of hundred ants, listening to the shovel ring dull against the scrubby bark-flaked pine. He swung the shovel up over his shoulder and made his way, through the heat, home.

From the path, he heard his wife calling out. He rounded the bend to see the house in front of him, the woman standing in front of it, hands cupped around her face.

"You seen her?" she called, this time to him.

"I haent seen," he said.

"Where in hell?" she said. He shrugged.

"What of that hoe there?" she said, pointing.

"I put it there," he said.

"What about it?" she said.

He shrugged. He walked over to the barn doors and pulled the hoe handle out of the rings, leaving a long streak of rust on it. He stepped inside and pulled the door shut. Hanging the hoe back where it went, he paced out the floor and started to dig, heaping the dirt against the wall. He pulled out shovelfuls, feeling the pressure in his back deepen the farther down he had to go.

Banging the shovel clean on the side of the hole, he hung it in its proper place. He sprinkled the bottom of the hole with hay, dropping in handfuls. He dug through the hay, pulled out the body, jaundiced now with grain dust. He kneeled, lowered it in, dragged with the shovel blade the dirt back in over it, stamped the grave down, kicked the rest of the dirt around the barn until it was no longer visible.

He put the shovel away. He left the barn.

The woman was standing on the stoop, looking out in the low, clear sun.

"What you been doing?" she said.

"Nothing," he said.

"Thinking?" she said.

He drew time out long, to figure her. "Thinking," he said

"About what?" she said.

"About nothing," he said.

"You know what I been thinking about?" she said.

"I can guess," he said.

"You think we give the sheriff a call?" she said.

"No," he said.

"You seen her?" she said.

"No," he said.

"You going to look for her?" she said.

He did not answer. He looked at what the sun was doing through the aspens. He looked at the way the stoop had grown worn underfoot, and at the difference in how the sun shone off the rough spots.

"Will you look for her?" she said.

"I will not," he said.

"Look at me to tell me," she said.

He turned to face her, turned all the way around, feeling his boots drag hard over the rough patches until he was facing straight at her. He opened his eyes all the way open and stared her in both her eyes. He looked at her in the eyes and looked at her, and looked at her, without blinking, until it was she who blinked and turned away.

Killing Cats

BRIAN EVERSON

They wanted to kill their cats, but the problem was the
problem of transportation. They invited me to dinner to beg
me to drive them and their cats out to the edge of town so that
they, the cat killers, could kill their cats. There was no need
for me to participate in the slaughter, they said, beyond
driving, nor any need for me to watch them kill their cats.
Probably it was better someone stayed in the car and kept the
motor running, they said. They did not know what laws
existed about people and their cats, about what people could
inflict, legally speaking, on their own cats. Nevertheless, they
assumed there were laws and statutes and ordinances, books
and books of legalities concerning felines and their acceptable
modes of death, they said. Laws and statutes and ordinances
which, they informed me, they were prepared to break.

I did not much care to try my hand at cat killing, but all I
would have to do was to drive. I did not have to kill the cats.
So I told them, yes, I would drive them, yes, as a token of
friendship–if they would pay for gas. They said all right, they
would pay, and introduced their cats to me. The mother
Checkers, the female kitten Oreo, the male kitten Champ.
They apologized for the banal names–although knowing what
I knew about these cats I was hardly in a position to establish
rapport. I would have preferred not to have known their
names. Better that they be for me just "the cats." I was only
the driver: all I knew, if questioned, was the road there and the
road back from there, nothing about what occurred at the
place itself. But the people insisted on telling me names, and
once they told me they insisted on apologizing, telling me the
cats' names were not names the people personally would have
chosen, but had been, they unfortunately insisted on telling
me, the names their children had chosen.

The man went to the hall closet and rummaged out a gun and wads of stiff, filthy rags. He rubbed the gun down with the rags. He polished the gun up and, after sighting down the barrel at me, handed me the weapon.

"Think it can do the trick?" he said.

I held the gun a moment, for form's sake, before returning the gun to the man. I said, yes, it probably would.

The man pointed the gun at the dining room table, telling me how sometimes, when he saw the cats climb up there to lick the plates, he wanted to "blow their furry bodies right off the table." He had wanted to "blast the cats away" for quite some time, he said, Checkers most of all, he said, but Oreo and Champ were no exception. Tonight was the night, he indicated. He pointed the gun and made a sound so I would know what he meant.

I watched the woman wander on tiptoe down the hall, peeking through doorways. She came back into the kitchen, started picking up cats.

"Sound as angels," she said. "Let's be on our way."

"Slugs, honey?" the man said.

"Honestly, dear, I haven't the least," said the woman.

The man returned to the hall closet. He opened the closet, kneeled down before it, thrust his hands in. He threw things out. He threw out metric wrenches and mason jars full of canned peaches, ski poles and winter coats and tangled scarves, Monopoly money and airplane glue and a milk-crusted glass. He surfaced with a fist-sized plastic box.

"Kids get to them?" the man said, holding the open box upside down, shaking it.

"Am I paid to watch them?" the woman said. "Honestly!"

Saved, I was thinking.

Not the cats–myself. I cared what happened to the cats only insofar as its happening affected me. Not that I have anything against cats, but people pay good money for their pets. They have a right to do what they want, as long as they leave me out of it.

"Perhaps the hardware store?" said the woman, looking at her watch. "Or Carl might."

"Charles? Jenkins, you mean? Old Chuck Jenkins?" the man said.

The man looked at the cats, spat into the shag rug.

"Cats like these are not worth the waste of lead," he said. "These three are dumpers."

The man demanded to know what I thought of the idea, the idea of dumpers, it being my car, me to be the one to get the ticket if things went awry. As long as he paid for gas and did the dumping himself, I told him, I was with him.

They sat in the back seat, stroking the cats, their faces fading in and out with the passing street lamps. The wife suggested it might be a nice gesture to give each cat a good solid crack with the pistol first, the butt end of it, for certainty's sake. It would be the kindest thing, she thought.

I told them please to wait until we were on the highway. There was no point in being premature.

There were three, they said to me, three cats, counting kittens as cats. They said they could not help noticing that there were three cats and three of us too, when they counted me.

I said, no, no need to include me, that was okay, not at all, but thank you, thank you, I really appreciate the offer, thank you for asking.

The cats screeched like power saws when they hit the pavement. I watched the man and the woman in my mirror, dropping cats. I kept watching afterward, watching them look out the rear window.

"Whoops," the man said. "Oh, no."

"What?" I said.

"Nothing," said the man.

95

"Awful," said the woman.

"Such a mess," said the man.

"Should have given them the smash," said the woman, hefting the pistol.

The man leaned forward, put his hand on my shoulder. He put his mouth close to my ear. I felt his warm breath.

"Drive back and finish them, buddy," said the man.

"It's the merciful thing," said the woman.

"Turn this rig around," the man said.

In the rearview mirror I watched what I could see of his face next to mine. He remained motionless, not speaking, the street lights flashing into and out of the car.

I kept driving.

"Be a friend to me in this," he said. He took the empty pistol from his wife and held the snout against my neck. "Aim for their skulls."

What I Know About Ham Ratchetslaw, Trombonist–by Clay Henry, World-Famous Beer Drinking Goat (Buy Me a Cold One Today at Inez's Trading Post, Lajitas, TX)

MATT CLARK

June 7, 1991

He did not come by stagecoach. Nor did he parachute down from a star-spangled bi-plane at midnight. He did not ride in by horse, camel, well-trained longhorn or Harley. There were no race cars or hearses involved in his arrival. Pogo sticks and tricycles are out of the question, considering the quality of local roads. The whole year round it is much too dry for canoes and submarines and Oxfordian punts and pontoons and steamboats and long trash barges, although he may have rafted in to Lajitas and walked over. (But not by himself. Not on *those* rapids. And *I* didn't see him go by.) No fighter planes were seen streaking overhead, and contrary to popular everyday life around here, no UFOs were spied in the immediate vicinity. No rickshaws. No locomotives. No army surplus helicopters. None of them brought him to town. Beats the hell out of me how he got to Terlingua, Texas.

*   *

I know only as much as Juan has told me. And a little bit more from the boys who laze around in front of The Trading Post, under the shed. And some from Mimi. Being a goat, it's tough to get any more information than that. Plus, I'm "stuck" in this pen.

I, of course, am not the first Clay Henry. And I will not be the last, by any means. Those punks in the pen over there constantly hope my liver will explode and they will be chosen to ascend my throne. We're not related. I'm not related to anybody that I know of. Not even the Clay Henrys who

97

preceded me. I'm not as alone as the glam-babies, movie stars and real-life heroes I hear on talk shows, though. Sometimes I lean in through the Inez's window to watch their staticky faces, to listen at their pathetic sob stories. "Having the world at your feet is an exercise in solitude," they whine at Johnny and Phil and Geraldo. No, I have my admirers, the tens of tourists who stop here to get a souvenir photo of Dad sharing a beer with me. I've never been on TV at all, but I can tell you if Oprah asked me to appear for even just one second, the first thing I would say is, "Fame is great." It was great before the whole Ham Ratchetslaw business, and it's even better now.

* *

Mornings go like this:

It's just before dawn and I'm awake. Thirsty. I see Juan off in the distance, getting closer and closer. The desert around Lajitas is not your level wasteland type. It's a roller coaster. Hills and gullies. The landscape undulates. So. Juan appears, jogging, then disappears He then appears again– at the top of another rise– and promptly disappears. It's three miles from La Kiva, where Juan tends bar, to here. Takes him about nineteen minutes, on average. I can only see him for the last two or three minutes, though. If the sun were completely up, maybe I could observe his approach a little longer.

"*Buenos dias*, Clay Henry," he announces chugging up to me, hands on hips, slightly bent over, gasping, sweating.

It's useless for me to try answering. I stare meaningfully. He gets my drift.

"What can I get you this morning, pal of mine?" Juan asks. Then he pauses like I'm talking to him–which I'm not– and nods. "You are watching your figure, you say?"–I didn't.–"And can only accept a Miller Lite?" He strides into The Trading Post and I hear him and Inez speaking. "This morning for Clay Henry a Miller Lite, Inez." I hear the door to the refrigerated display case slide open, the cold air

98

streaming out, the door gliding shut again, Inez telling Juan he's crazy as shit.

Call me a hedonist or a drunk or whatever you want, by now my mouth is watering and my lips are quivering madly. I'm hooked, I'll admit it. But hey, that's my job. I'm Clay Henry.

Juan comes back outside with the Lite and a grape soda for himself. He smiles at me, and I'm sure he thinks I'm smiling back at him, the way my mouth is acting. "*Una cerveza* for my best *amigo*, my last customer of the night, Clay Henry," Juan says. He opens the beer and hands it over the fence. I wrap my lips around the top of the can and turn it up slowly, chugging. I don't miss a drop of it and wind up the performance by dropping the can back over the fence for Juan to pick up and put in the recycling bin. We're big into ecology around these parts.

"How was that?" Juan asks and waits for my non-reply. "Oh, really? That good, you say? The perfect way for Clay Henry to kick off another day in the limelight?" At this point I will either belch or give a short bleat to show my thanks and dismiss Juan. He has to jog back to his trailer behind La Kiva, and I have a full day of tourists awaiting.

That's what it's been like every morning for the last five years, since Juan took up jogging. And that's the way it will be tomorrow morning. And the next. Mornings will be that way until my liver pops and I fall over dead–yeah, shut up you boys over there; I'm fine for now and you'll end up barbecued, the lot of you! *Cabrito*, you hear?–or until Juan decides to give up jogging. The only time mornings have ever been different, I guess, is during the Ham Ratchetslaw Affair and immediately thereafter, when Mimi would jog with Juan.

*   *

According to the boys under the shed, he walked into the Chevron Diner just after sun-up, wearing a white linen suit with an pumpkin-orange tie. He carried a long, black case that he gingerly put into a booth before sitting down, handling the case like it was full of money, the boys say.

Mimi recalls that his shoes were very clean. "Too clean for around here," she tells me. "And he was skinny." A fairly normal condition around here.

Mimi says she said, "What can I get for you this morning?" because she is the waitress *and* the register girl until Juno comes in around eight. And the stranger told her he wanted nothing but a Big Red and a pickle.

So, Mimi says, she knew something was up with this guy.

"Hey, Mimi," the boys under the shed call out. They're taking a break from patching rafts. "What do you want to go painting Clay Henry for? No goats in France?" (Mimi came over here from France to paint. She didn't COME here to paint, really, but was just on a tour of the Southwest and when the bus stopped in Terlingua–just outside of Big Bend National Park, not far from me and Lajitas–she got off and decided to stay and become a painter. In France, she'd been a napkin folder for a tiny, five-star hotel.)

"Clay Henry," Mimi coos, "you pay them no attention. You are much more than a goat. And beautiful? You are gorgeous. Perfection. You hear?"

When Mimi scratches me just between my horns, I'll admit it, I get a smidgeon turned on. Maybe we goats are a little on the sexual side, I don't know. Mimi is a beautiful French woman and I am a farm animal turned superstar. It would never work out, of course.

Plus, Juan would kill me.

*　　*

"I am a trombonist," the stranger is now rumored to have announced in the middle of the Chevron Diner. As if the occupation were some kind of charm to ward off the stares of everyone eating their hash browns and *huevos rancheros*. (With only 37 people total living in the Terlingua/Lajitas area, you can't blame people for gawking.) And so, I am told, each person in the Chevron bowed their heads and looked only at

100

the plates in front of them while they tried not to smack or swallow too loudly. The place was deathly quiet. Possibly for the first time in its existence.

"He was mortified," Mimi explains. "So I finally thought to say to him, 'A trombonist! Why that is marvelous. You know we have a blues combo here in town that could use a trombonist.' That made him feel a trifle better, I believe. And then other people said to him that what I had pointed out was true, that he should go out to the ghost town and wake up the blues combo and see about joining them. They were scheduled that very night to play at La Kiva.

"And you know what, Clay Henry? The man smiled at me and said he loved the blues as much as his father loved rain on a sunny day. I don't know what he meant, but it made me shiver."

"Us, too," the boys under the shed chime in, crossing themselves. "We all shivered when he said that."

"You know, we should all pitch in and buy a new pool table," one of the raft boys suggests. Five of them are sitting around with their feet propped up on the old table. It's missing two legs and a hen has built a masterpiece nest on its precarious slope.

"Let Inez pay for it," another one of the boys protests. "It's her joint."

From inside The Post, Inez hollers, "I'm not buying a new pool table. I too much enjoy the eggs and quiet that one produces now."

Knowing better than to argue with Inez, the raft boys one by one pretend to drift off into sleep.

*   *

Rocky and Pete and Ringo, the blues combo, do not come to The Trading Post anymore. Not since they broke the pool table. Thus, I do not know what it was like when the trombonist went to visit them at their home in the ghost town jail. I don't even know what they look like anymore, they

101

have all grown so, I am sure. When they were eighteen, last year, I could out chug all three of them.

*　*

Being a Friday night, La Kiva was packed, I am told. The Rangers from the Park came and the people vacationing in the Park came and the hippies from the commune came and the citizens of Boquillas and San Viciente and Castolon came, as well. Juan has told me they sold three times as many margaritas as normal and four times as much beer. He leaned close to me and whispered, "Mimi danced barefoot, my friend, and I stopped serving drinks to watch for just a moment the way she moved like a breeze through the river willows."

*　*

I heard the music and was impressed. I have listened to Rocky and Pete and Ringo rehearse from the beginning and it has been a very slow thing, their improvement. But that night, with the trombonist sitting in, taking long rambling solos that flew away from La Kiva's patio over to me and Inez at The Trading Post–I cannot describe to you how much it seemed like something magical was transpiring there, across those three miles.

Inez doesn't sleep, you know. She stays up all night and listens to recordings of the Dorseys in their prime, and their prime, I am telling you, was nothing compared to the sounds this trombonist was conjuring up. Inez came outside and sat on the top rail of my fence, scratching the tip of my nose, making my tail squirm. "Clay Henry," she said, "what is happening over there?"

*　*

"Whirling and spinning and clomping and jumping and swaying and twisting and bouncing and shimmying and leaping and shaking and bumping and hopping and flailing

102

and shuffling and moving. It was a miracle you should have seen, Clay Henry. The whole place dancing like they were possessed, like Ham Ratchetslaw's music had turned us into the kind of spirits you'd find flitting around Prospero's island." Mimi told me that.

Once, a long time ago, she read me *The Tempest* by William Shakespeare, changing her voice for every character in the play. Soft for Miranda. Brash for Prospero. Low and sad for Caliban. There was a splendiferous ending, I remember, but I was confused by its abruptness. I wanted to know—and I still do—what became of Caliban when they all got back to Milan. In civilization was he abused? Or admired? Showcased or scorned? Did he ever get over Miranda and fall in love with a comely young monster? Did he get to "happily ever after" too?

*   *

Apparently, amidst all the revelry, nobody noticed the first armadillo arrive, or the second or the third or the three hundredth. Nobody noticed all the armadillos, the *thousands* of armadillos, until the band's snaky version of "Mona Lisa" stopped and the kind of silence that can only be made by a crowd overtook La Kiva. They were surrounded. Besieged and encircled by football-ish dinosaur remnants.

"It was like a painting," Mimi whispers, standing up from where she sat, waving her hands in the air as if to color the scene for me there in the chill winds coming in off the Chisos Range.

*   *

Two days later all of Terlingua was still awash in armadillos. And at the town meeting, after much discussion among the citizens and a confused and confusing talk by one of the Park's Rangers, Ham Ratchetslaw stood up on the top of a booth in the Chevron Diner and said: (according to the boys under the shed)

103

Good people of Terlingua, the plague that has come down on you is both unusual and unpleasant, possibly unhealthy. Leprosy and all that. You cannot do anything without the armadillos finding a way to do it with you. They claw their way through doors to join you in your showers, listen to your phone conversations, attend to you while you make love to your respective spouses, brutalize your geraniums and green beans. In truth, they sit amongst you even now, *here*, in the middle of your comfortably distinguished town hall and diner. What could have caused this most ludicrous circumstance? you ask yourselves and this very learned man from our nearby, understaffed but radiantly superior National Park. Why has this horde of armored pests been visited upon this town? I'm afraid that I have the answer to your questions, my comrades. In fact, I *am* the answer.

(An uproar ensued that Ham Ratchetslaw quieted with a few notes on his slide trombone. The people and the armadillos pricked up their ears, both large and fleshy and small and spiky, to listen.)

It's my music. The music you enjoyed so much the other night in your snazzy cantina is responsible for the presence of the beasts. Drawn to it like junebugs to a streetlight, doubloons to the ocean's floor. Unable to drag themselves away from the heat and gravity of the blues. I've had it happen before. In different places. Different animals, too. Salamanders, rats, and in one terrifying instance, elephants.

(Here Ham Ratchetslaw was interrupted by a chorus of "what-can-we-do?s)

Well, I'm the one that got you into this mess. Certainly I can be the one to get you out. To be sure, I did not count on this happening way out here in the desert like this. But I swear I will rid you of the dreadful boogers. Oh yes, no matter how excruciating that exorcism may be I will not

rest until the armadillos have been driven one and all from your village. Though it may cost me my life, I will do what must be done.
(At the end of this vow, it has been related to me, Ham Ratchetslaw stood atop a booth, trombone in his left hand, right hand reaching ceilingward. He was posing, I suspect, but the trusting and flustered denizens of Terlingua were as mesmerized by Ratchetslaw's oratoria as they were by his melodic interludes. One of them, as if on cue, shouted out not "Hallelujah!" but "We'll pay you."

Ham Ratchetslaw remained motionless. Someone else added, "We'll pay you 1110 dollars," which just happened to be the amount the town had saved up to install picnic tables at the top of Mule Ear Butte.

His arms lowered first, then his face. The smile of Ham Ratchetslaw beamed out over the Terlinguans like the sweep of a Hollywood searchlight. Inez was told—and she told me that the trombonist's teeth and lips didn't move a millimeter. Nevertheless, he could be heard loud and clear when he announced, in a sepulchral tone:)

You've got yourself a deal.

*   *

I saw them.

First I heard the music. Then I heard them. Then I saw Ham Ratchetslaw—the first sight poor Clay Henry had of the villain—riding in the back of Ringo's jeep, charming the armadillos to follow him down the road, past The Trading Post and off toward Ojinaga. Their little claws, thousands upon thousands of them, clicked against the hilly asphalt of I70 like a castanet cult. He played "Oh Susanna," and "Peggy Sue," and "Goodnight, Irene, Goodnight" and ran them all together in a bizarre medley that made me itch to climb over my fence and join the 'dillo's lemmingish parade.

105

Then they were gone. Apparently to be lost in the wilderness or sold off to Mexican craftsmen who might kill them and teach their corpses to stand very still, holding tiny musical instruments and miniature pieces of sports equipment. (You'd be surprised at how tourists will spend their money in these wild environs.)

*   *

When Ham Ratchetslaw returned to Terlingua late that afternoon, the whole town was holed up in La Kiva celebrating the blessed exodus with shots of Cuervo Gold. Juan has explained to me that the first shot was on the house. Everything after was happy-hour priced.

Six o'clock. Sun's running out. Hen Egg Mountain glowing like the progeny of some charmed goose. Mimi and Rocky and Pete and Juno from the Chevron, all of them, everybody, drunk as skunks. And they'd been thinking aloud and loudly with one another and comparing notes and deducing like wildcats. They'd decided in a sort of reverse People's Choice Award election, that the toast accompanying the first shot of tequila ("To our hero, Ham Ratchetslaw!") should be rescinded and replaced with something more curse-like. The new consensus was that they had been had, and they were not in the least bit happy about it: Ratchetslaw had brought the 'dillos to town purposefully, so the poor Terlinguans would be forced to pay his extermination fees. La Kiva was a bar full of pissed and highly pissed amateur sleuths. There was spit and talk of extortion and lynching on every set of lips: a road-crew passing through volunteered a trough of hot tar; Virgil Rivas promised to pluck every chicken in his possession. "We'd be fools to pay him," Moe Grunyon slurred, and I am told that a salt-lick/lime-suck toast was being made to just this decision when Ham Ratchetslaw entered La Kiva with a cased trombone and a calligraphied bill for services rendered.

*   *

106

I was standing on the big rock in my pen, just under the sign which proclaims me to be the "The World Famous Beer Drinking Goat," trying to get a grasp on the uproar at La Kiva. From across the miles of cacti and rattlesnake tracks I could hear shouting and four short screams. Then the roar of cars starting up and high-tailing it in as many directions as the two roads leaving Terlingua permit.

When Caspar Anaya pulled up to tell Inez what had happened, I leaned in through the window of The Trading Post to listen to him. "'If you don't give me my due,' Ham said, 'I'll take whatever I like.' Then he pointed a finger at Mimi and said, 'I like *you*.' And before anyone knew what was happening, he was gone. Like a roadrunner. Vanished in the desert. With Mimi tossed over his shoulder like a sack of French dog food. They're trying to organize a search party right now."

*   *

Getting out of the pen was no problem. It was the walk that almost killed me. I'm not used to walking much, you know. So. By the time I got to the door of Juan's trailer, I was exhausted and my hooves ached. I scratched at his door with the tips of my horns until he came to the window and looked out at me. He'd obviously been crying, and I wondered how many people had witnessed these tears.

"Clay Henry!" Juan exclaimed. "What are you doing here?"

I bleated at him, but he misunderstood me completely.

"This is no time for beers, friend. Mimi has been abducted by that damnable trombone player. She is nowhere to be found."

I barged up the metal steps of the trailer and pushed my way past Juan into his living room. A framed picture of Mimi was sitting on the coffee table and I poked it with my nose, then looked back at Juan. He was watching without any understanding in his eyes, just ignorance and misery, so I poked the picture again. (Mimi climbing out of the Rio

107

Grande at La Cloncha, wet and laughing, a bottle of Cuervo clutched tight against her bikini'd chest.) Then I walked to the bookshelf, pulled out a copy of *Lassie Come Home* and nuzzled its cover over to Juan's feet. I bleated again, hopped out of the trailer and stood facing north, sniffing.

*   *

The trail was simple to follow. But long. It rambled beside Terlingua Creek for close to 14 miles before we stood at the bottom of Packsaddle Mountain (elevation 4661 feet). The scent of pickles and Mimi's Tea Olive perfume obscenely mixed pulled my snout up toward the top of the mountain until I zeroed in on a small cave almost hidden behind a wall of stalky succulents. My howl, more a consumptive cough than collie's wail, communicated my success to Juan. Up there was Ham Ratchetslaw, trombonist, and his captive, the woman that Juan and I loved more than Patsy Cline, the dainty French painter my best friend intended to marry.

*   *

When we went back to Terlingua to gather forces for an attack on Ham Ratchetslaw's hideout, Juan and I met with some unexpected cowardice. In the eyes of the town's citizens, a stock of people who reveled in the unrelenting heat and desolation of Texas's Big Bend area, who wallowed in the mysticism that floated around the park in hippie vans and reports of ghost lights, Juan and I both detected the dull sheen of fear. I could smell it, too. Sour and rotting. Unpleasant as smoldering wigs.

Miles Elton, a ranger who had retired from the service rather than face charges of peyote harvesting, explained the situation to Juan like this: "The devil, you see, he was tossed out of Heaven, right? For acting so high and mighty. A talented boy, I guess, if God felt some kind of threat from

him. Sumbitch landed on a mountain hereabouts, was
repulsed by the beauty of the valley he saw and flew off to
Ojinaga across the Rio. Spent his days bouncing a big metal
ball on the heads of anybody who dared to step outside their
home. You've seen that ball, Juan, in Ojinaga, dusty and
immovable on Saragossa Street. Sumbitch dropped it when
the town's priest came back from a visit with the Bishop and
started chasing the old bastard around with a cross. Routed
him all the way back to the mountain he'd landed on to begin
with and left him trapped in a cave on top of that peak.
According to legend, the padre left the cross guarding the
entrance to the cave, and Satan's been huddled inside ever
since, bemoaning his ill fortune and the loss of his big metal
ball."

Juan fidgeted in his seat, not touching the enchiladas Juno
had set in front of him. "Well hell, Miles, I know that story.
What does that have to do with Ham Ratchetslaw and Mimi?"

"Juan," Miles said, "you can't tell me you don't see the
connection. Ham Ratchetslaw is the very devil himself. Soon
as you told us about that cave, we all knew. Grew up on the
tale, we did, wondering in our beds at night where that
mountain cave was, whether *El Diablo* spent his cross-tapped
life watching the roofs of our houses, longing to drop his ball
through shingles onto our dreaming noggins. You can't
expect us to go tromping up there and tangle with the devil,
Juan. We're lucky he left at all," Miles said.

Juan stood up. "But he took Mimi. And you can't
honestly tell me you think some scrawny trombonist in an
orange necktie is the master of Hell." He looked around at the
tops of people's scalps and baseball caps. "You can't tell me
that."

After a few seconds of silence, Juan spit on the floor and
said, "I'm not afraid." He walked to the door of the Chevron
and turned back to look at me eyeing the beef jerky jar on the
counter. "Come on, Clay Henry," he commanded.

I ate *The Bible* once. A little red one. Given to me by a
woman running away from her evangelist husband with a
photographer from *Life*. Almost choked to death on this
passage from Leviticus:

> And Aaron shall lay both his hands upon the head of a
> live goat and confess over him all the iniquities of Israel
> and all their transgressions in all their sins, putting them
> upon the head of a goat and shall send him away by the
> hand of a fit man into the wilderness.

What a scary book!

*   *

I led the way up the mountain to the mouth of the cave. Juan
followed close behind, carrying no cross, no garlic, no silver
bullets, no rosary beads, no *Bible*, no votive candles, no St.
Christopher medal, no vial of Holy Water, no glow in the dark
Jesus Frisbee. Nothing. The boy came to confront a man who
might easily be the Dark Lord and held nought but a canteen
of Gatorade and a flashlight loaded with store-fresh Duracells.

(I might have mentioned this before. I was still drunk
from a Winnebago of college boys that stopped by The
Trading Post just after sundown. On their way to the Rio to
raft. Spring Breakers. Generous fellows. Outstanding
chuggers. One of them nearly beat me.)

*   *

Juan's flashlight beam reached into the cave and got eaten
alive by the darkness. "Ham Ratchetslaw?" Juan said. There
was not the kind of echo late night movies lead you to expect.
"Mimi?" The silky name sank to the slick floor
without bouncing around even once.

I followed Juan deeper into the cavern, winding our way through a toothy squadron of stalactites and stalagmites. "Clay Henry?" Juan said, and I grunted to let him know I was still in tow. "Clay Henry, I think maybe there is something out of the ordinary about this."

Duh.

Ahead of us we could see a light coming from around a corner, yellow, flickering. "Look," Juan hissed unnecessarily.

The bartender-turned-devil-hunter took a deep breath to muster up courage. I did the same. The smell of guano was strong, but floating above that was the scent of Mimi's Tea Olive, ridiculously out of place in a batshit maze. With a small bleat for encouragement, I nudged Juan in the ass to make him go, and we rounded the corner to meet our fates.

* *

Nobody said anything.

Juan didn't say, "Mimi!" or "Ham Ratchetslaw, you fiend!" Ham Ratchetslaw didn't say, "Impertinent mortal!" or "Curses! Foiled again!" Mimi didn't say, "Juan! My hero!" or "You've come at last!" or "Kiss my foot." The only sound in that cave was the hiss of a citronella candle that swayed in the breeze Juan made as he walked over to Ham Ratchetslaw and yanked the spit valve off the end of his trombone's slide. He took Mimi by the hand and they walked side by side out of the light, the way we'd come in.

I stayed but a moment, searching Ham's candle-lit eyes for some semblance of recognition. Goats have long been unfairly associated with Satan, but Ham looked at me without the faintest glimmer of mythically conspiratorial hope. He looked at me like a man who has just lost his car on a bet he could outchug a barnyard beer guzzler. When I turned to leave, he didn't rise to follow or fight or turn himself into a pointy-winged, drippy-fanged demon. He kept his seat and with trembling digits fingered his now-useless mouthpiece.

111

Trotting up behind Mimi and Juan, I heard very clearly Ham grieving. His trombone's melodies were ruined. No longer crisp and sharp, the music that leaked out of Ham's abyss was marred by the fuzz of air escaping from a massacred spit valve. All the way home I heard unbearable renditions of "Sweet Adeline," and "Rose of the Rio Grande." He tried his damndest to play "Mrs. Robinson," and the pitiful sound, a mixture of brassified flatulence and all-too-human weeping almost made me feel sorry for the man. I don't believe there's anything more depressing than a miserable trombonist.

*   *

Mimi stands up to turn the canvas and easel around for me to see. I stick my head through the fence's rails to get a close and critical perspective on the piece. It's a portrait of me sporting the medal I was presented at the Mule Ears Butte Picnic Table Dedication Ceremony and Clay Henry Appreciation Day. My horns glisten like steel. My hair is neatly arranged. Even my beard looks good, streaked with strands of distinguished gray. I am mightily impressed with what a handsome creature the artist has made me out to be.

Standing that close to Mimi I suddenly realize once again people don't tell goats everything. Some news items we must sniff out for ourselves. Like the future. Like babies underneath salty flesh. Twin boys to be named Clay and Henry, asleep with a portrait of me hung above them. Mimi won't find out the news for another week or so. Then Juan will jog over to tell me before anyone's parents are phoned or college funds discussed. He and I will share a Miller Lite in the first rays of a Friday sunrise, pleased that the winds carry no music, only the last cool fragments of a clear Chisos night, and the promise of babies laughing in the desert.

112

Two Photographs by Walker Evans

JOSH RUSSELL

There is a Walker Evans photograph that no one save my
family and those who visit us has ever seen. In it a man stands
in a barbershop doorway, his face half-covered in lather,
half-shaved. The pole bisects the image. Captured in the bold
tones of all of Evans' work, it looks like peppermint candy.
The barber, his name on the plate glass like a caption, is
perplexed as he holds his razor over an empty chair. The
harlequin man in the doorway looks right into the lens. His
hands rest on his hips. He glares. The man is my father and
this is the story.

Evans took a photograph of my sister Lillian, at
seventeen. In it she lies nude on a bed covered with a simple
white sheet. Her hair is a crazed dark crown on the pillow and
her foot casts a shadow like an ink stain. Her legs are parted
and her vulva is captured in those wonderful gradations of
black and white of which Evans was a master. She showed
the picture to me the day she packed, though I was a
thirteen-year-old boy and knew nothing. The sight of her
naked was shocking and beautiful. While she filled a musette
bag with her things she told me how the photograph came to
be taken. She and Evans were lovers, and one morning when
my father and I had assumed she was shopping in the Quarter,
Evans had simply taken a playful snapshot of her as she lay in
his bed. They had just made love and she pointed to the smile
she wore in the picture as proof that she was happy there with
Walker. Evans had left shortly after the photo was taken, and
she was supposed to catch a bus on the sly and meet him in
Valdosta, Georgia. The last days he was in New Orleans
Evans had feared murder by my father's hands. Searching her
bureau for forbidden Lucky Strikes, my father had happened
upon the photograph of his daughter basking in a bliss whose

source no one could fail to recognize. The next day, mid-shave in a Royal Street barber's, he spotted Evans as he snapped shots of a grocery. He raced to the door and yelled Walker's name. Evans turned with his camera to his eye and saw my father through the lens. He snapped the shutter reflexively; the composition was too good to waste–a cat sat on the edge of the frame, in the window combs and scissors swam in a jar of antiseptic, the daddy of his lover stood scowling with his face half-masked by shave cream. The next moment my father was sprinting across the narrow avenue and Evans was running for his life, cutting down Pirate's Alley and ducking inside the St. Louis Cathedral on Jackson Square. This picture of my father hangs tacked to the wall in the front room of his small house uptown on Magazine. A Western Union boy brought it to him the day after Lillian was gone, two days after he'd received half a shave. There was no note, only Evans' studio stamp on the back of the print. As far as I know, I am one of only four people who have ever seen the picture of Lillian-Evans, my father and herself being the other three. Why show it to me? I asked, amazed that she had. Love, she told me, is the most important thing in the world. Everyone will admit to this, but I want to tell you something they won't: Love is the body. Believe the body, she said. That's why I'm showing it to you.

Bloodlines

DIANA JOSEPH

My father was a tall man, and when he was young, he'd been whip-skinny. Now his stomach pouched out–hard fat–and his arms were thick and strong from pounding nails into horses' feet. Horses were his passion. He was partial to Appaloosas, a flashy breed, those loud spots. He liked to look out the window and watch them grazing in the pasture–green grass, blue sky, spotted horses. When they ate the grass down to stubble, he stretched a rope across the lane and let them graze in the pasture. He liked to look out the window and see a horse looking back in.

For a few hours each afternoon, my father let the Quarter Horse stud out of its dark stall and put it in the southern pasture. There was an oak tree growing in the middle of the pasture, and the stud was killing it, chewing off the bark and gnawing right into the trunk. Horses will do that sort of thing when they get bored: chew on trees, crib wood fences, jerk down their feed buckets. It gets to be a habit for them, but one you forgive–like smoking.

Sometimes, my father propped me on a wood fence, leaning his body against mine so his left hand was free to hold his cigarette, and his right hand was free to offer half an apple to a horse. He blew smoke into the horse's face until it sneezed and I laughed. *Tabby Cat,* he'd say, *someday, you're going to ride a horse.*

In western Pennsylvania, August is a humid month. The humidity wraps its sticky arms around you and licks the back of your neck–that damp place under your hair. We lived on forty-seven acres. We had horses and dogs. We had a barn that my father built.

My father hunted white tail buck. When he was fifteen, he killed a twelve point. Its head hung on a wall in our living room. Its eyes were made of glass. That gun that killed it was in the living room, encased in wood and glass.

The gun in the barn was meant for killing large rats and stray dogs, fearless raccoons with foaming mouths; my father kept it hung on the wall next to the saddles and bridles and bits. He was a steady shot.

Horses fall hard when they are shot. Stall boards splinter and crack, give in to their weight. Dust rises out of their coats. Their eyes stay open.

On a Saturday morning in August, my brother died, and my father shot every horse in the barn: five Appaloosa mares, one Quarter Horse stud, one paint pony–seven bullets. He hurled his gun across the fence, into the pasture, and he took off running, his steps high and clean, graceful–as if he'd practiced running like that. As if he knew where he was going.

That afternoon, men and boys who knew my father and my brother came to our farm. I stood at the high window in my parents' bedroom, my chin level with the ledge, my mother just inches away, but still out of reach, as she wept quietly into the telephone. She was calling people and telling them that Martin had died, Martin was dead. She was sitting on the edge of her bed, her eyes were closed, and as she talked, she rubbed her fingers in tight circles like she did when she had a headache.

I stayed at the window. I watched those men and boys walk up the lane. Loggers and Amish Dutch farmers, high school football players, mechanics and carpenters. They carried chain saws and crowbars, hammers and rope. They pried off and cut through siding boards to tear down the walls of the barn. They wrapped rope around dead horses's stiff legs and dragged them out of their stalls, trailing blood and flies. One man hitched the paint pony's legs to my father's tractor and pulled it out. *Rigor mortis,* he said. Another man knew a guy who worked for the county and convinced him to bring their backhoe. None of them seemed to know where my

116

father had gone or when he'd be back, but it didn't really matter. They were still going to bury those horses.

Earlier that summer, my mother waved a hair brush at me, and I backed into a corner like I was terrible afraid of her. I wasn't, of course; I was just showing off for my father. *I'm good and sick of fooling with you, Tabbitha,* she said, but I slipped past her, hiking up my nightgown so I wouldn't trip. I *don't want you to brush my hair, I told her. I want that guy*–I was pointing at my father–*I want him to do it.*

And he did. He unwound my braid and gently brushed out my hair, counting off every stroke, one to one hundred and one, unlike my mother, who cheated, skipping numbers as if I wouldn't notice.

My brother had a wavy mop of uncontrollable hair. He wanted his bangs to cover his forehead so he tried to tame them by holding them down with pieces of masking tape. He came into the kitchen like this on the morning he died. My mother put down her coffee cup. *Come with me,* she told him. She led him into the bathroom, and when they came back out, the masking tape was gone, Martin's bangs laid flat and heavy, and he smelled like Aqua Net.

That summer, something mysterious was happening to the drinking glasses. They kept breaking, clean breaks that snapped away from the rims. We didn't know it at the time, but it was my mother's ring. When her soapy hand circled the inside of the glass, the diamond cut through.

My mother's ring was a present from my father: a diamond fifteen years too late. It was a guilt gift: my father bought the Quarter Horse stud without telling her he was going to.

My mother didn't love horses. Not the way they smell–of sweat and hay and manure. Not the way they buck and snort, the way they chew on your leather shoe strings. She didn't love the way their hair drifts across the floor in the barn, is carried by a breeze through the air, is brought into the house on your clothes. She was afraid of horses. When my father

117

was in the barn, she stayed in the kitchen. Maybe she looked out the window, toward the barn, full of longing. Was she remembering the woods, making love with my father on his deer stand–before horses became his passion? Did she hold a glass under steaming water, tap it lightly against the faucet, and wonder why it cracked?

She loved my father. These are the things she would forgive him for: head of a buck suspended on the wall, calloused fingers snagging her green silk blouse, son conceived on a deer stand.

She said, *Men will only be as good as you let them.*

My brother and I watched my father work the Quarter Horse stud. He put it in the cross ties and touched it: pinching its nose, lifting each leg, rubbing its belly. He put it on a lunge line and ran it in tight circles. Left, then right, then left again, flicking the whip at its feet. My father beat the Quarter Horse stud: with the handle of a pitch fork, his whip, a branch from an oak tree. The stud backed into a corner of its stall and trembled at the sight of my father but it never looked away from him.

My father laughed. *He thinks he's a tough guy,* he said. *He thinks he's tougher than me. But watch this: I can move him with my head.*

When he tilted his head to the left, the stud stepped left; he tilted right, and the stud stepped right.

How'd you do that? my brother said. *Will he do it for me?*

My father said, *Only for me. It's because he hates me.*

My father and brother bickered over whether I should have a pony or a small horse. Martin thought ponies were short on patience and full of spite. *Ponies bite,* he said. *They kick. A pony will throw her off first chance it gets.*

Who are you? my father asked. *Sir Knows-a-lot?*

My brother loved horses, but he wasn't a good rider. He didn't trust a horse when he was on its back. I never saw him ride anyone but Colter, my paint pony, a gelding, fat and stubborn. Martin had to help me saddle him: Colter had a habit of puffing himself up as soon as he felt the weight of the saddle. The minute Martin cinched the girth, Colter relaxed, exhaling noisily, causing the saddle to slide loose. *Goddamn pony,* he'd mutter. He'd ride poor Colter hard, snapping the reins against his neck and hips until white sweat lathered up. By the time I got on Colter, he was too exhausted to give me any trouble.

Twenty years since I've been on a horse, but I'm still a good rider.

You don't forget.

On the Saturday morning in late August that my brother died, my father got up late. After French toast and sausage links and silence that lasted until he drank several cups of coffee and smoked two cigarettes, he asked my mother if she knew what Martin's plans for the day were. She was washing breakfast dishes. She said, *He's in the barn.* My father said, *I've got fence post holes I want him to dig.* He let the screen door swing shut behind him, not bothering to close the heavy door–it was a morning cool for August, but it would get warmer and eventually hot, humid–and the dogs were barking, and you could hear country music coming from the barn radio, and a horse was kicking against its stall, and a horse whinnied, and the others answered, and when my father came back, he stood outside the door and shouted through the screen: *Call an ambulance!*

My mother didn't hear him. She was stooped over, dumping wet coffee grounds into the plastic bucket she kept under the sink–she spread all sorts of scraps over her tomatoes. *What?* she said.

Don't ask me what. Do it. Call the ambulance.

Then he was gone.

He'd found Martin in the barn. Martin in a stall, gate slid shut. The Quarter Horse stud standing on his arm. The Quarter Horse stud putting back its ears and showing its teeth. The rising smell of piss, the dogs' pink tongues, a steel guitar

119

solo, and Martin already dead. Kicked and stepped on. Already dead. When the ambulance arrived, my father had the stud horse in the cross ties, and with cracks of his whip, he'd bloodied its nose and belly and legs and ass and genitals.

I counted seven shots.

Through a window, I watched my father run, becoming very small.

Where was he going?

My mother said she didn't know.

Then she said, *You want your dad?*

The keys to his truck were on top of the refrigerator; she took them.

She said, *Let's go get him, Tabbitha.*

She knew exactly where to go. She drove down the lane, turning left onto Bowden Road, another left onto a dirt road that led us through neighboring hayfields. When the dirt road ended, we got out and walked. Neither of us said anything. Mosquitoes swarmed thick in the air; crickets were chirping; that eerie purple-gold dusk streaked across the sky, and every time you blinked, the sun dropped a little further. Our shadows were long and narrow. We found him sitting on a hickory stump under his deer stand, his elbows were resting on his thighs, his hands were covering his ears, he was looking at the space between his feet, and I have seen men sitting this way since—in airports and bus stops and train stations, at this very moment on the edge of my bed; men broken by bankruptcy and faithless wives and their children's hate—and I hate when men sit so huddled and hidden and defeated. Men will only be as strong as you let them. When my father looked up, he said, *I knew you'd find me. I knew you'd come.*

The Dress

DAVID EBERSHOFF

It was summer and I was ten. My father said he and my mother would be gone for two hours, out pricing washing machines. "Watch the castle for us, King," he said, his arms spilling appliance brochures. My sisters, Dorrie, Dottie and Debbie, were going over to swim at Sarah Minnihan's, whose parents had just dug a pool into their hillside yard. The pool's redwood deck hung like a balcony over the arroyo, Debbie had reported, impressed. "Yes, but do they have a dumb waiter?" my father countered proudly, as if ours had run in twenty years.

Our driveway was on a hill and hooked like a backward S. From the upstairs hall window, from behind the orange Roman shade, I watched my father back his putty-colored car down the drive. The car slowly rolled onto the dry lawn, chewing a patch of dirt, and I could see my mother in the passenger seat look up from the hole of her purse and cheerfully tell my father he was on the grass. "I know that, dear," his lips mouthed, the color draining from his face.

My sisters followed, down the drive in swimsuits with beach towels wrapped around their waists and heads. Their plastic high-heel sandals clacked against the pavement like the silver bells that fell from the eucalyptus.

Then they were all gone.

The house was both big and hot. A widow, Mrs. Homer, died in it during a September heat wave, forty years after her husband had built it for her. When I was in the second grade my dreamy, awkward-limbed father–unable to fathom why such a hulk of a house would sit on the market for eighteen months–bought it from her estate, which was more than happy to rid itself of an earthquake-prone brick house that needed work in all twenty rooms. But after three years in the house, my father had made almost no improvements. The lilac-and-

121

trellis wallpaper from 1912, waterstained and peeling, still hung in the den. In the bedrooms the original rose-colored carpets remained, stains of wear ground into the nap. The house's brass doorknobs and keyholes, unpolished in a generation, were as black as rot. And there was a third floor, mysterious in its distance from the parts of the house where we lived, with four bedrooms connected by a dark hall with a wood floor sticky with disintegrating varnish. In Mrs. Homer's younger years the top of the house served as quarters for a household staff. Now there was nothing up there except the original black corrugated rubber mats nailed to the floors and, in one room, a circle of metal folding chairs arranged by my father in an attempt to furnish what he could not afford.

As soon as I was sure my parents and my sisters were really off, I climbed the back stairs. The summer heat was trapped up on the third floor, as dry as the gold hills I could see from the little oval-topped window at the top of the stairs. Although it once scared me–Dorrie said Mrs. Homer collapsed to her death up there–I'd learned early that the third floor was the only place in the house I could sit and read and not hear my sisters' voices rising and rising like engines only finding higher gears.

There was a deep closet with a sloping ceiling still filled with canvas garment bags and satin-wrapped hangars holding Mrs. Homer's clothes. There were two cedar drawers filled with cream kid gloves and lemon satin pumps and even a white ermine stole, its rodent mouth hinged as a clasp. Dorrie, Dottie and Debbie liked to play there, hauling into the room with the circle of metal chairs armfuls of tea gowns. They would dress each other and their many friends, who were often sisters themselves, their six, ten, twelve girlish voices confidently loud. Occasionally I'd quietly slip into the room, timidly joining their laughter and excitement over Mrs. Homer's outfits, observing the unstated rules of play. I would hold up a dress to a sister's chest when it seemed the right time, suggesting the right felt bathing-cap hat to match, until one of their faces, usually Dottie's, would freeze icy and hard, and she'd say, as if it had just occurred to her, "But you're not a girl." An embarrassed silence would follow, until someone, usually one of the friends, would say, "Yeah." And then again, from someone else, "Yeah."

I went to the closet. It was even hotter in there, the air smelling like the red clay of a baseball field. I pulled from the back metal pipe a dress I'd seen one of the friends, Sarah Minnihan, in fact, try on a month or so ago. It was green gingham with eyelet trim and an empire waist. Its moon-white satin sash was long and rubber-banded into a fat roll. Sarah had wrapped her waist with it and then crisscrossed it over her chest, delicately denting the cushions of her breasts, tying an enormous bow at the top of her spine. She placed her fists on her hips and began to strut up and clown the hallway that connected the rooms, turning every few feet in tight hard circles, the puppy ears of the bow flopping against her back. Dorrie said she looked dumb, but I was growing wide-eyed, a sweet, dirty wow of a thrill running across my skin like a shiver. "This is what debutantes wear in West Virginia," Sarah Minnihan said knowingly, with such confidence that no one, not even Dottie, dared to suggest she was making it up.

The third floor's empty, dark rooms were perfect for dressing up and dancing, for bustling about, for hurrying from doorframe to doorframe like a soprano singing her ails. Perfect for playing except for one thing. There was no mirror. And that was all the fun, seeing the dress twirl, seeing my pale thin arms hug the bodice, tucking my genitals behind my dosed thighs and then lifting the skirt to see the empty triangle of my crotch.

I took the dress to my parents' bathroom, the only room in the house with a reliable lock. It was larger than my bedroom and had two pedestal sinks and a green rubber floor trimmed, all the way around, with a strip of white vinyl. In its day it was the fanciest bathroom floor money could buy, my father told me the day we tried to impossibly scour the gray stains out of it. It reminded me of the squeegee blade I used to wash the front windows, shredded and smelly. At the far end of the bathroom was my mother's claw-footed tub. Its inside was scabbed with rust, but when filled it looked like a calm, glass-green pond.

I began to run the water and then pulled off my clothes. My briefs were clingy gray, the elastic waist a little saggy. In the mirror I noticed my long legs, a promise Dr. Deputy had reported, of the height to come in my teens. They were smooth and golden, a solitary freckle on the inside of my left thigh. My brown nipples were uneven and oblong. They reminded me of the pennies my father and I flattened on the train tracks at the corner of Del Mar and Raymond. Oh, how he would hunt the gravel for the smashed coins, searching in the night with the patience of a hound, while I hung onto the car door, ready to go home, wondering why he even brought me at all, wondering if he was silently acknowledging that it really didn't matter if I was there or not.

And then I slipped the dress over my head. It didn't fit well, tight in the chest and reaching only mid-shin, but I chose not to notice the absurdity, the fact that it looked as if I were wearing a pillowcase. To me, it looked like an elegant gown, and I an elegant if naive girl. When I thought it–*you look like a girl*–nothing in me shuddered with loathing or fear because I hadn't yet discovered those outgrowths of the self. I rightly knew that I was playing, and that I wasn't; that the impulse to dress up and dance meant nothing, and that it meant something. I loved looking like a girl, although I knew I wasn't one, because it somehow brought to life for me the vague, ticking-away feeling that I wasn't a boy either, or at least not like the boys in my class, that I was exactly what Sarah Minnihan had said when she caught me clasping a purple bead bracelet around my wrist: "Why, you're not a boy," she stated, neither shocked nor angry. "You're a girl-boy."

124

My father kept a short-wave radio on the windowsill that he listened to while shaving. When I turned it on, a lady was singing, her voice a twinkle of birdsong. From the bathroom window I could see across the arroyo to the neighborhood of eucalyptus and cypress trees where the Minnihans lived. I thought I spotted the blue flash of swimming pool tucked into the dry hill, but I wasn't sure if it was theirs, so many were being dug these days. The lady on the radio suddenly stopped singing and there was a silence filled with the sounds of shifting audience. Then another woman began, her silvery voice reminding me of the night earlier in the summer when my father took just me to the Hollywood Bowl to hear the last scene of *Siegfried*. When Brunnhilde woke from her icy slumber, singing her first words *"Heil dir, Sonne!"*, a blow of terror knocked the breath out of me. When the soprano, a tiny Norwegian with red hair, opened her mouth, the thunder-clap sound rifted me open, the notes dragging tears from my eyes, and I had never felt more exposed to my father. I was both hurt and shocked that he would bring me to something like this. It almost seemed obscene, the enormous, squared 0 of her mouth yanking from me strings of private emotions, my fragile self splayed out in front of my father like a set of entrails. All the while my father sat happily, swaying slightly, his finger playing the conductor's baton. When I looked at him and he turned to greet my stare with his bucktooth smile, I cautiously stood from the bench and backed my way out of the row and then ran to the car, incredulous that people could listen to music like this and ever face one another again.

I went to the mirror at the back of the door and unrolled the sash. I wrapped it around my waist three times, sucking in my little pad of a gut so that it girdled my middle. I'm an hourglass, I thought, admiring my waist which cinched up to something no bigger than a thigh. Then I threaded the two ends of the ribbon between my legs from behind, wrapped my belly again, and knotted the sash at the small of my back.

125

The first lady came back on the radio, this time singing something that made me think she was even sadder than before. I twirled myself when her voice lifted and sank to my knees when I was sure she was singing, crying really, about despair. In the mirror I watched myself attempt to mouth the words, my small, open lips nowhere near synchronizing with the voice. But I didn't care, for the music and the dress–the freedom to play, to curtsey and to clutch my breast, to arch my eyebrows and press my fingertips to my lips–the rare, uninterrupted moments of an afternoon to pretend and dream provided me with the fun I failed to find on the soccer field, or anywhere else. "So what?" I sang in my closest imitation of the lady's voice, which had become a violin-induced trickle, as if she were dying, but not dead yet, and just as I shut my eyes and parted my lips to sing a few more notes with the dying lady, just as my throat began to relax and produce my girlish head voice, a fist landed on the door and a pip-squeak of a voice called out, "Hey, Drew, what're you doing in there?"

My eyes snapped open to the suddenly garish sight of myself bound in satin and gingham.

"Drew? You in there?"

"Yeah."

"Hey, Drew, it's me"

"Who?"

"What do you mean who? It's Rex. I came over with the girls." Rex Minnihan was a grade ahead of me and was the type of boy whose crooked teeth were always jutting from an optimistic smile.

"I'm taking a bath," I said, disoriented and now resentful that my one chance in weeks to play was barged in on.

"Get out of it. I came over to play."

I began to walk in a circle of hurt. I blamed my sisters for betraying me by bringing Rex over, as if they'd known not to leave their little brother alone even for an hour, as if I might hurt myself. There was nothing to do but dismantle the

126

afternoon. "I'm coming," I called as I began fiddling with the sash. As it turned out, I'd tied the knot tighter than I realized. Picking at it began to hurt my fingertips. I shouldn't have knotted the sash where I couldn't see it, I thought, my elbows out as my hands continued fussing at the nook of flesh above my ass.

"Drew, what's taking so long?" Rex began to bang on the door, the mirror shaking in its doorframe.

"I'll be out in a sec."

"Why don't you just let me in?" The doorknob began to tremble, and my fist jumped to my eyelet neckline and began clawing at it. What was Rex trying to do to me?

I twisted the sash so that the knot was at my navel. Maybe I could wiggle out of this thing. I tried to roll the belts of ribbon down over my ass, but they jammed at my hips. With the sash bunched up over my groin, it looked as though I was wearing a pair of panties over the gingham dress, or a diaper. The ribbon pulled between my legs was now bunching up on the tiny white peach of my scrotum. The pressure on my testicles was a deep purply pain, so buried it almost felt like it was happening to someone else. The sinking feeling in my chest was equally remote, as if I profoundly knew that, in spite of the immediate terror of Rex working the door knob harder and harder, I was not so lame that I could get myself inextricably tied tip in a green gingham dress. In fact, the thought of it–*But nothing like that would ever happen to a Bruder!*–my father would often cluck–calmed me, and I said, "Rex, go downstairs. I'll be out in five minutes." From nowhere I had pulled the tone of a woman snappily putting the brakes on her kissy man, and my instant resourcefulness gave me enough of a steady head to press my palms flat in the air and think, Now, let's get out of this old thing.

Rex had apparently slinked away, silence coming from the other side of the door. I moved closer to the mirror to inspect myself, lifting the skirt to see the grape-stain impressions the tight sash was leaving on my skin. The dented flesh looked raw, and I began to worry about scarring and about what invention I would have to create to convince my wife–for even in this predicament it did not occur to me that I would one day love a man–of the pure origins of the bluish tissue slashing my hips and inner thighs. I was born this way, I could tell her with a face so stony and impenetrable she would never dare bring up the subject again. Yes, it would be a useful excuse for many things to come, I realized, gracefully held in a still instant of revelation in my parents bathroom with the green rubber floor, my skirt scooped up in my arms. What on earth could anyone say to such a comment? It would cut off all argument, it would silence my opponents, and just as I was beginning to think I had discovered one of the major maps to my life, a crashing thud landed against the door, stretching it as if it were made of taffy. And then another came. And then another.

"When are you coming out?" Rex barked, his hard little body flinging itself against the door again and again. "Are you dead? I came over to see you!"

I stood back, my fingers madly working at the knot. I desperately pulled my arms out of the sleeves and shimmied the bodice down my chest. I began to yank on the skirt, feeling the sash cinch tighter and tighter with each pull. Then a sharp crack! eased through the doorframe. As Rex's floppy cowlick appeared from behind the door, I swooped up my tea-length skirt and hopped, feeling like every nineteenth century heroine I'd ever seen on the run, across the floor and into the tub. By the time Rex was all the way in the bathroom, I was standing in the bath, the wet dress hanging from my waist, limp, sheer, and unerotically sad.

Rex's face, his freckles dark in the late summer, froze in confusion, as if this would have to be explained to him later. I smiled pathetically, my hands spread modestly over my crotch. He just stood there, his mouth ajar, his left hand

128

trailing delicately back to the doorknob. "Sorry," he muttered, his voice so shaken I knew he wasn't on his way to tell all.

When he was gone I didn't have time to nurse my indignity. I tried to relock the door, but the bolt was hanging like a loose tooth. Wet, the sash's knot was smaller and tighter, and I became so enraged by its lock that I began to rip at the dress. I'm not sure why I didn't think of this sooner but probably because, even after Rex's visit, I was slow to realize that my play day had been spoiled. At first, nothing seemed ruined and so I hardly felt like shredding to streamers Mrs. Horner's dress, which I might want to wear again. In fact, I was more frustrated with the sash itself–I was convinced of a fault in the original design: who would need such a long sash anyway?–than horrified by the predicament I'd created for myself. And so now I wanted to get back at those unruly yards of ribbon and, because they wouldn't budge, the apple green gingham was the next best thing.

Before long the dress was hanging in strips from the tenacious sash, which now wrapped the small box of my loin. The ribbon was as thin and dingy as a shoelace, its taut lines pressing into my red skin. All my tugging had shimmied the knot down to a few inches above my penis, which I noticed, as one detachedly notices a tick on the leg, was hard. It was no longer than a key, and about as shiny. What it was doing I had no idea. My only other erections thus far had come accidentally when I was lying on my stomach in front of the television on the gold velvet sofa, the knuckle-sized lump in my shorts snuggled arousingly into the soft V of the two seat cushions. And the more I strangled the sash's knot the longer my penis held firm, its tip beginning to ache.

"Everything okay, King?" I could hear my father breathing on the other side of the door. "Rex said you might need my help?"

It was a question I wished I had years to answer. Did I need his help? Would it be worth it? But I didn't have the luxury of time to weigh every implication of bringing in my

129

father or not. I was still stuck in the remains of a dress and the hard wet sash was beginning to hurt. I *did* need his help, more than ever, and a wave of ill-timed reasoning swelled inside me and I thought to myself, But isn't he still my dad?

I covered myself in his green terry robe that was hanging on a hook by the shower. The robe was like a dress itself, or an outer coat, with a matching sash hanging in belt loops. It was too big for me, my hands lost in the sleeves. When I opened the door and emerged, my father, his hands in his pockets and his heals rocking, simply asked, "All clean, Kingaroo?"

I walked through the sitting room that connected my parents' bathroom and bedroom. It was empty except for a lone file cabinet, an indication of my father's plan to one day convert it into an office.

Their bed was made with a navy blue blanket with an aqua satin sash. I sat down on the edge. With his lips pursed he shrugged his shoulders and lifted his eyebrows: "Drew, you're forgetting we're copilots. If something's eating at you, then tell me. What's the secret password?"

"Bess Truman," I mumbled.

"Bess Truman it is!" He clapped his hands and then prodded, "Kingaroo?"

"Yes?"

"What's wrong?"

"Nothing."

"Nothing what?"

"Nothing, Prince Dad." With that, I again felt the terrible grip of the old wet sash. My father was still standing in front of me, only closer now, my eyes looking into his stomach. Their room smelled like carpet shampoo. Panes of afternoon sun were landing on the rug and I held my breath as a wave of shame swept through me, and then moved out. "I can't get out of it," I finally said, loosening the robe's belt and slowly peeling back its shoulders.

130

My father's face stopped in time. "King?" he said, his voice a whisper's sigh.

"The knot's too tight." And we both looked at the grimy fist of sash, like a grotesque outey belly button. But even more startling than it was my sturdy little erection, persistently defiant and appalling, just below.

Suddenly, as if someone had snapped their fingers in front of his face, my father said, "Let me get the door." He began rubbing his hands together as he often did before beginning a project. "We'll have you out in no time," he said, pacing in front of me, his eyes aimed at the floor.

With my elbows propping me up, I sat on the bed, my chest pushed out and my legs spread. I was beginning to shed my embarrassment, as if the cloying sash had also numbed any sensible reaction to such exposure. I simply wanted him to get on with it, to break through the knot I could not, and when he at last crouched between my thighs, his huge hands delicately avoiding the red drippy tip of my penis, I realized that the reason I could no longer feel my shame was because it, all of it, had transferred to my father, where it sat in lumps in his broken-heart face. At first I thought he was going to ask me how this happened, but then, as his fingers picked hopelessly at the knot, I saw that he wasn't going to be able to bear the details. He already knew more than a father would want.

"I was just playing, Prince," I ventured. He didn't say anything for about a minute, his head bent in a painful mixture of concentration and confusion. He had straight brown hair with strands of gray sprouting from the crown, and I felt the regrettable urge to reach out and stroke it. When he felt my hand on his neck, he looked up from his toil, his eyes drooping and watery. It was then I knew what he thought of me, what he would always think of me, how the green gingham dress would be as closely associated with me as the color of my eyes or my love of music, and that even decades from now he would view me from the sides of his eyes and

131

wonder how his seemingly upright son was spending his dark, private, incomprehensibly perverse hours.

Oh, I couldn't stand it. I flopped back on the bed and shut my eyes. It was there that I lay for another few minutes that crept by like hours. It was there that I felt my father's hand graze the pipe of my penis and listened to him mutter a terse, angry "Sorry." Lying on my back, my father nudged my legs open wider for more work space, and at that my eyes rolled back into my head and I silently begged for a future without the dress. I would do anything to be rid of this whole day, I told myself. Anything to get off the bed. And when my father rather belatedly said, "I'm just going to cut this damn thing, I swelled up with relief thinking that at last it was over, at last I could sit up and leave my parents' room. He snapped a pair of scissors through the sash, saying, "We'll just have to forget about this." I was at last free, and I put on his robe again and nodded with eager agreement as I left his room, certain that forgetting was a realistic option. For I was ten and my father was a man who whistled when he backed his car into a pole; we were both made of happy hope. There was no reason to think that I would be lying on my parents' bed in a ripped dress with my father between my legs for the rest of my life. There was no reason to believe the humiliation would last any longer than the sash's red weltish marks. It was over. The welts in fact were dying down.

But an hour later, when I was dressed and downstairs and saw my father across the kitchen counter, he and I both knew where we were. I was back on my back on his bed. And during the next week, when I passed him in the halls of the rambling empty house, he would look at me, his mouth twisted as if he didn't know what to say, and I would be sent back to the bed, to my receptacle position with the growing feeling it was the only place I belonged. And when, the following Saturday, he found me on the third floor thumbing through Mrs. Homer's closet, searching for an ivory silk shift Dorrie and Sarah Minnihan sent me to find, he simply said,

132

"Drew, please," and simultaneously we shuddered, the two of us bereftly aware that our relationship had been reduced to the few minutes on his bed. "When are you going to stop this?" he begged, turning away. And I couldn't blame him, for neither of us could handle the untying of another dress's knot– once seemed enough to endlessly stupefy. We were counting on the months to pass quickly to lessen the bind of a harshly clear memory, pleading for time to pick up the pace of its slow, ineffective healing. But every morning his blank face at the breakfast table continued to send me back to the bed. His turning his back as we changed in the swimming pool's locker room flung me back to the blue blanket. His careful knock before entering my bedroom told me where, in his mind, I still lay. And so, before any peace had settled, it was back again to the edge of that bed.

Not even a month had gone by, but this time it was with my sisters, the four of us lined up–Dorrie, Dottie, Debbie, and then me–our feet swinging anxiously, while we watched our grandfather, my father's father, shuffle into the room to tell us with an older version of the broken-heart face that he, his only son, a man who loved his children very much, a man who wasn't prouder of anything in the world than his three daughters and his only son, Drew Jr., was dead.

"What did you say?" Dottie asked, her face turning blotchy with grief.

"Your father is dead and done gone," my grandfather said. "Let him remember you as you are."

133

ACKNOWLEDGMENTS

A.E. STALLINGS **The Man Who Wouldn't Plant Willow Trees** *The Beloit Poetry Journal* **A Lament for the Dead Pets of our Childhood** *Poetry*

BRIAN HENRY **Insomnia** *The Prose Poem: An International Journal*

JAMIE SIMPSON **Spectators** *The Laurel Review* **Guest Stars** *The New Orleans Review*

SEAN THOMAS
   DOUGHERTY **Gratitude** *The Christian Science Monitor*

JACK B. BEDELL **A Fair Share of Morning** *Louisiana Literature*

CARRIE ETTER **Sacred Ground** *Zone 3*'s **The Birthmother's Handbook** *Ascent*

LAURA LEE
   WASHBURN **Beard Lady's Circus** *5AM* **Dying** *Weber Studies*

KARLA FRANK **Numb** & **The Race** *The Literary Review*

MICHELE
   GONZALES **China** *The Literary Review*